Take Hold of Your Future

Leader's Manual

JoAnn Harris-Bowlsbey
James D. Spivack
Ruth S. Lisansky

Towson State University Counseling Center
Towson, Maryland

Published by
The American College Testing Program
Career Planning Services

©1982 by J. Harris-Bowlsbey, J. D. Spivack, and R. S. Lisansky. All rights reserved.
Except for specific instructional use by a course leader, no part of this book may be reproduced in any form or by any means without permission in writing from the authors.

ISBN 0-937734-03-9

Contents

Introduction 1

Session 1 7

Session 2 17

Session 3 21

Session 4 31

Session 5 49

Session 6 53

Session 7 61

Session 8 73

Session 9 77

An Optional Approach to Sessions 10 and 11 82

Session 10 83

Session 11 87

Session 12 91

Session 13 99

Session 14 107

Appendix A Class Handouts 113

Appendix B Paper Graphics 121

Appendix C Exercise 4B—Exploring Occupations by Assessing Your Interests ... 137

Appendix D Course Syllabus Chart 141

References 143

Introduction

Purpose of the Program

The overall purpose of the Personal Life and Career Planning Program is to increase the vocational maturity of the individuals who participate in it. Thompson and Lindeman (1981) have enumerated six factors of vocational maturity: (1) awareness of the need to plan ahead, (2) decision-making skill, (3) knowledge and use of informational resources, (4) general career information, (5) general World-of-Work information, and (6) detailed information about occupations of one's preference. The Personal Life and Career Planning Program addresses all of these factors and, in so doing, attempts to teach skills which can be used again and again as individuals make new choices in successive life stages. In addition, several sessions are devoted to the collection of self-information—specifically: interests, skills, abilities, and values. This self-knowledge becomes the basis for generating a list of personal occupational alternatives which will be used in a practice problem directed to learning about occupational and educational resource material.

The six themes of vocational maturity are treated in different ways. Awareness of the need to plan is enhanced through learning about the Life-Career Rainbow (Super, 1980) and through interviewing individuals in one's chosen occupational field. Decision-making skills and strategies receive major attention in Session 2, and the rest of the program develops a planful model for personal vocational decision making. General career information is presented through the Life-Career Rainbow instruction in Session 3. General World-of-Work information is also introduced in Session 3 and continues throughout the program through development of concepts illustrated in the World-of-Work Map (copyright 1977 by The American College Testing Program). Use of occupational and educational resources and the acquisition of detailed occupational knowledge are emphasized in Sessions 10 and 11, as participants research specific occupations by reading, interviewing, and using available media and computer-based systems. Since vocational maturity can be defined as *the ability to cope adequately with the developmental tasks of a given life stage,* the long-range goal for individuals in this program is to develop the ability to use the skills introduced here to cope with career decision making in later life stages. The short-range goal is to enable them to make a sound preliminary vocational choice and related educational decisions.

Target Populations and Methods of Delivery

The Personal Life and Career Planning Program has been developed for adults of postsecondary age. The material is appropriate for use with high school seniors, community college students, four-year college and university students, and the segment of the general adult public in search of a vocational choice or change. The program has been extensively field-tested as a two-hour undergraduate university course.

The program is laid out as a systematic set of materials for use in fourteen two-hour sessions (see following Syllabus Chart). It was principally designed as a two-hour credit course for the community college or four-year college or university. Alternatively, the program may be used in its entirety as workshop material for an adult group, or particular parts might be selected for this purpose. If offered as a credit course, the assignments, the final project, and the pre- and post-testing of decision-making skills are appropriate. If offered less formally (as a group workshop experience, for example), the assignments may be modified and testing eliminated.

Personal Life and Career Planning Program
Course Syllabus Chart

Session Number	Content	Step of Decision-making Process	Suggested Activity/ Homework Due	Date of Session
1	Overview of program Administration of evaluation instrument Introduction to decision making			
2	Decision-making problems Group decision-making experience	Step 1: Identifying the problem	Read Chapters 1 and 2 of the *Career Planning Guide*. Complete Exercise 1, Decisions List, to be handed in.	
3	Life-Career Rainbow	Step 1	Read Chapter 3 of the *Career Planning Guide*.	
4	Self-concept and career implications	Step 2: Gathering information about self and environment	Read Chapter 4 of the *Career Planning Guide*. Complete Exercise 3, Vocational Self-Concept Questionnaire. Begin to read biography or autobiography of a famous person.	
5	Organization of World of Work Internal factors influencing vocational choice: interests and skills	Step 2	Exercise 4A, Exploring Occupations by Assessing Your Interests. Continue reading biography or autobiography and write report (due in this session).	
6	Internal factors influencing vocational choice: abilities	Step 2	Complete Exercise 5, Exploring Occupations by Assessing your Experiences and Skills, of the *Career Planning Guide*.	
7	Identifying occupations related to personal interests, abilities, and skills, and experiences	Step 2	Score CPP Abilities Test	
8	External factors influencing vocational choice: stereotypes	Step 2	Read Chapter 7 of the *Career Planning Guide*, and complete Exercise 6, Stereotyping in Employment, with either of the two options described.	

(Continued)

Syllabus Chart—*Continued*

Session Number	Content	Step of Decision-making Process	Suggested Activity/ Homework Due	Date of Session
9	External factors influencing vocational choice: career information	Step 3: Identifying alternatives	Read Chapter 8 of the *Career Planning Guide*.	
10	Occupational research	Step 4: Weighing the evidence	Complete Exercise 8, Occupational Research Sheet, of the *Career Planning Guide* for five occupations.	
11	Occupational interviews	Step 4	Interview at least one of the two people listed on the Occupational Research Plan Sheet. Use Exercise 9, the Occupational Interview Sheet, for doing so. Be prepared to discuss this interview in the next class session.	
12	Narrowing occupational alternatives	Step 5: Choosing among alternatives	Work on final projects.	
13	Career Action Plan Identify major or program of study Resume writing	Step 6: Taking action	Read Chapters 9 and 10. Complete Exercise 10, Preferred Job Characteristics and Values, of the *Career Planning Guide*.	
14	Review of program	Step 7: Reviewing the decision and consequences	Prepare to give oral report to class on individual project. Write up project to hand in.	
15	Final exam (if desired)			

Materials and Format

The Personal Life and Career Planning Program—"Take Hold of Your Future"—consists of two companion publications: this *Leader's Manual* and the *Career Planning Guide*. Although the *Leader's Manual* is integrally tied to the participants' use of the *Career Planning Guide*, the *Guide* can be used as a self-contained unit by an individual who belongs to no formal class or study group.

The *Leader's Manual* has a standard three-part format that generally applies to each of the fourteen sessions:

1. *Summary*—A cover page that summarizes (a) what the leader needs to do to prepare for the session and (b) the activities, suggested timing, and materials for the session.

2. ***Objectives and Activities***—A detailed description of objectives and suggested activities for the session.

3. ***Background***—Essential theoretical material for the leader (not required for all sessions).

Appendixes A and B contain master copies for class handouts and/or paper graphics; the leader may remove these to make copies for the class or transparencies for overhead projection.

History of Development

The Life and Career Planning course was initially developed at Towson State University in response to a need to provide—given minimal investment of resources—career guidance services to a large number of individuals. Career guidance materials were organized into an academic course format, then submitted to and approved by the Academic Curriculum Committee of the University in 1974. Careful attention was given to maintaining the integrity of the career guidance component as well as the academic rigor necessary to ensure quality education. The course was instituted as a formal two-credit academic offering, applicable as an elective toward graduation.

Extensive field-testing has been conducted at Towson State over a seven-year period. During the first year, a total of six sections were offered, with a maximum of twenty students per section. By 1980-81, eighteen sections were offered. Enrollees have included returning older students as well as full- and part-time traditional-age students. To serve a broad spectrum of student types and needs, the course has been offered during the day, in the evening, and also in the summer.

After each academic year, a coordinating committee of Counseling Center staff has revised the course content and format based on feedback and evaluations from students and leaders. In addition, since 1978 The American College Testing Program (ACT) has provided a number of reviews while considering publication of this material. The current product reflects critical analysis of both structure and materials by Towson State University Counseling Center professional staff and by independent career guidance professionals engaged as reviewers by ACT.

Systematic evaluation has been an integral component of the program. Using formal assessment measures, students have consistently shown increases in (a) *career maturity* (Crites—Career Maturity Inventory), (b) *career decisiveness* (Osipow—Career Decision Scale), and (c) *use of a rational decision-making style and specificity in selection of a college major* (Harren—Assessment of Career Decision Making). Students who have completed the program have provided the following evaluations on a five-point scale (5 = excellent, 1 = poor):

    Specification of course objectives — 4.2
    Attainment of course objectives — 4.0
    Overall course evaluation — 4.0

These figures represent cumulative means of student ratings in approximately 25 sections of the course (total of 500 students) from the fall 1980 through fall semester 1981.

Based upon the same cumulative student rating, leader effectiveness was rated 4.0 and leader knowledge 4.2. Since many of the sections were taught by counselor interns with no specialized knowledge of career development and guidance, this *Leader's Manual* apparently succeeded in supplying the cognitive background needed to teach or lead this program.

Selection of Leaders

An effective leader for the Personal Life and Career Planning Program must be able to handle both the presentation of lecture-didactic material and the coordination and processing of small and large group exercises. Counselors with facilitative skills and sound knowledge of career development and choice theory and practice should have the knowledge and skills to be effective leaders. Also, because the materials are so complete and structured, professionals from other disciplines can be trained to utilize the material effectively. It is strongly advised, however, that nonguidance professionals have inservice training or, even better, serve as co-leaders with guidance professionals through one sequence of the program.

Planning Ahead

Since some of the exercises and activities in the program require advance arrangements, the leader will have to plan ahead. The specific requirements are described in the appropriate sections of the *Leader's Manual*. Here are a few helpful general suggestions:

1. For Session 6, order copies of the Career Planning Program (CPP) Ability Test Battery. Available from The American College Testing Program, P.O. Box 168, Iowa City, Iowa 52243 (telephone: 319-337-1349).

2. For Session 2, order group decision-making exercises (e.g., Desert Survival, ELM, Plymouth, Michigan 48170) or alternative exercise.

3. Prepare desired transparencies (see Appendix B) in advance.

4. Duplicate handouts (see Appendix A).

5. Invite guest speakers well in advance.

Selection of Facilities

The Personal Life and Career Planning Program employs three instructional modes: classroom-type lecture and discussion, large group activity and interaction, and small group activity and interaction. The facilities chosen for the program should be capable of accommodating all three. If the transparencies that come with the program are used, attention should also be given to the space requirements for audiovisual equipment and to means for darkening the room.

Program as College Course

If the institution has not had such a course for credit before, the first task is to get the content and the concept approved by the curriculum committee. The authors of the program have included significant cognitive content in the curriculum so that its worthiness for college credit can be easily recognized. Weekly homework assignments, the final project, and optional examinations enhance the academic credibility of the program. The program is flexible enough that additional content and assignments could be included at a local site in order to make the program more "academic," if needed. Clues for doing this are found in the *Leader's Manual* where resource materials are listed for leader preparation.

At Towson State University, where this program was developed and field-tested, students are graded on the basis of the completion of homework assignments and the final project. The points are allocated as follows:

Session	Assignment	Points
2	Exercise 1	5
4	Exercise 3	5
5	Exercise 4A	5
	Report on autobiography or biography	15
6	Exercise 5	5
7	Score CPP	5
8	Exercise 6	5
10	Exercise 8	20
11	Exercise 9	5
13	Exercise 10	10
14	Final projects—oral, written	20
(15)	(Optional final exam instead of project)	(20)

Total = 100

Since attendance is crucial to benefiting from the program, points are subtracted for absence. The University's usual standards for spelling, punctuation, grammar, and general neatness in completion of assignments were applied.

Session 1
Summary

Objective	Suggested Activities	Suggested Time	Materials
1. To provide a basis for measuring program effectiveness and progress of individual participants	Administer evaluation instrument, if desired.	30 min.	Copies of instrument Pencils Answer sheets
2. To provide an overview of the program and of leader expectations	Give an overview of the course, content, methods of participant evaluation, and course requirements.	15 min.	Course Syllabus Chart Additional local handout about grading policies, if desired
3. To provide an opportunity for members of the group to get acquainted with one another and with the leader	Do one or two optional get-acquainted exercises.	15 min.	5 x 7 cards Marking pens
4. To provide an introduction to decision making	Mini-lecture: Deciding Strategies Discussion of decisions made this week Develop criteria for effective decision making.	35 min.	Paper graphics 1 and 2 (Appendix B)

Homework

Read Chapters 1 and 2 of the *Career Planning Guide*.

Complete Exercise 1, Decisions List, to be handed in.

Supplementary Readings

Dinklage, L. B. *Adolescent Choice and Decision Making: A Review of Decision-Making Models and Issues in Relation to Some Developmental Tasks of Adolescence.* Cambridge, Mass.: Harvard University, 1966 (ERIC No. ED 010 371).

Gelatt, H. B., Barbara Varenhorst, and Richard Carey. *Deciding* (student's book) and *Deciding: A Leader's Guide.* New York: College Entrance Examination Board, 1972.

Gelatt, H. B. "Decision-Making: A Conceptual Frame of Reference for Counseling." *Journal of Counseling Psychology*, 1962, 9.

Jepsen, David A. "Vocational Decision-making Strategy-Types: An Exploratory Study." *Vocational Guidance Quarterly*, 1974, 23, No. 1, 17-23.

Resource Materials

Career Development Inventory (CDI) by Donald E. Super, et al. Instrument and manual available from Consulting Psychologists Press, Palo Alto, Calif.

or

Career Maturity Inventory (CMI) by John Crites. Instrument and manual available from CTB/McGraw Hill, Monterey Park, Calif.

Objectives and Activities

Objective 1: To provide a basis for measuring course effectiveness and individual progress

Suggested activity:

Administer one of the suggested evaluation instruments, if desired. Explain to participants that this instrument is being given in order to evaluate the effectiveness of the program and will have no bearing on evaluation.

Suggested time: 30 minutes

Materials: Copies of evaluation instrument
          Answer sheets
          Pencils

Objective 2: To provide an overview of the program and of leader expectations

Suggested activities:

A. Using the Syllabus Chart and material on pages 2 and 3 of this manual, the leader provides an overview of the 14 sessions in the program.

B. The leader provides information about the nature of the assignments (which are included in the *Career Planning Guide*) and talks about the methods of evaluation in the program.

Suggested time: 15 minutes

Materials: Course Syllabus Chart (copy from Appendix D)
          Any additional desired handouts concerning grading policies

Objective 3: To provide an opportunity for the members of the group to get acquainted with one another and with the leader

Suggested activities:

A. Arrange group into a circle. Distribute 5 x 7 cards and pass felt-tip marking pens around. Ask participants to put first names on one half of the card, to fold it, and to stand the card up on the desk so that other students can see it. Then ask individuals to relate one life incident or to describe something about themselves (interests, activities, things they do well, value dilemma, etc.) which will help other participants to know them better. It is suggested that the leader also participate in this exercise.

or

B. Ask participants to develop a short list of things they would like to know about one another, such as present career plans, educational background, name, etc. Place these items on the board as individuals suggest them. Then ask the group to break into *dyads* (pairs). One member of the dyad interviews the other about these topics for 3-4 minutes.

Then the other member interviews his or her partner. Participants are then asked to introduce their partners and to share the information which they have gained about that person during the interview.

Suggested time: 30 minutes

Materials: 5 x 7 cards
            Marking pens for activity A only

Objective 4: To provide an introduction to decision making

Suggested activities:

A. *Mini-lecture—Deciding Strategies.* The leader provides a brief overview of eight decision-making strategies and of any other decision-making material that there is time for. Group participants will read this material as the assignment for next session.

B. The group leader asks participants to share some decision, either big or small, which has been reached in the past week. As group members relate some decision, the leader asks three questions:

    1. What kind of *process* did you use in making this decision (from the eight strategies just reviewed)?

    2. What were the *outcomes* of your decision?

    3. Were you pleased with the outcomes?

C. After hearing several decisions and processes described, the leader asks participants to develop criteria for "effective" and "ineffective" strategies of decision making. At least two criteria should be offered:

    1. That the decider maintain control or assume responsibility for his/her actions

    2. That the decision strategy produce some action of a positive nature

After the criteria have been developed, participants are asked to place the eight strategies along an "effectiveness" continuum. The continuum might look something like this one:

```
Ineffective _____ Effective
        Paralytic                                    Planful
        Delaying                                     Intuitive
        Fatalistic          Agonizing                Impulsive
                                        Compliant
```

Ask participants to weigh the advantages and disadvantages of each of these strategies, and have them assess each strategy in terms of the degree of its effectiveness. Further, ask individuals to think about the kinds of decisions which might lend themselves to the differing strategies. For example, it might add spice to life to choose food or clothing by use of the impulsive strategy; the intuitive strategy might work well for choosing a friend.

Definitely draw some conclusion to the effect that the higher the consequences and the greater the degree of risk related to a given decision, the better it might be to make use of the planful decider strategy. *Although the planful strategy does not ensure positive consequences, its use does increase the probability of desirable consequences.*

Suggested time: 35 minutes

Materials: Paper graphics 1 (Factors in Vocational Maturity) and 2 (Impulsive Decider model)

Homework assignment: Read Chapters 1 and 2 of the *Career Planning Guide*. Complete Exercise 1, Decisions List, to be handed in.

Background

Program Overview (Objective 2)

The Personal Life and Career Planning Program has two overriding purposes: (1) to increase the level of vocational maturity of participants and (2) to assist them in making two important decisions: the choice of a vocational or educational program of study and the choice of an occupation. The first purpose is comprehensive and future-oriented; the second is specific and present-oriented.

Super (1974) indicates that there are at least six factors in vocational maturity: (1) awareness of the need to plan for the future, (2) decision-making skill, (3) knowledge about and use of informational resources, (4) possession of career information, (5) possession of World-of-Work information, and (6) possession of detailed information about occupations related to one's interests. The Personal Life and Career Planning Program addresses each of these six factors. Vocational maturity can be viewed as the possession of a set of skills to be used whenever vocational decision making is required. A major goal of this program, therefore, is to develop skills which can be used repeatedly in future decision making.

The second purpose of the course is to assist participants to use acquired skills to make two specific decisions: (1) the choice of a vocational or educational program of study and (2) the choice of an occupation. These choices are set in the context of information about self and environment. They are also viewed as tentative choices which may be altered.

As is evident from the Syllabus Chart, the program is organized around the steps of a planful decision-making process. The vocational choice is presented as a pertinent "practice problem" for the planful process, which should be applied again and again to life's significant decisions. By so doing, the authors underscore their belief that decision making is the central skill required for both career planning and personal life planning. The topic of decision making is addressed early so that the concepts involved can be reinforced through practical applications introduced throughout the program.

Following the study of alternate strategies of decision making (Session 1), the program presents a comprehensive description of *Career* (Session 3) as the interaction of all life roles in order to assist the participant to understand more clearly and perhaps define more precisely the nature and complexity of the problem of vocational choice. The information-gathering stage of the decision-making process focuses first on self-information. Based on Super's (1963) thesis that "the choice of an occupation is the implementation of a self-concept," Session 4 addresses the self-concept. Sessions 5, 6, and 7 assist the individual in specifying vocationally-related interests, aptitudes, and skills, and in relating them to specific occupational titles. Each of these is used to identify regions in the World of Work, a concept explained in detail in Session 4.

Sessions 8 and 9 direct attention to external factors in the environment, which must be compromised or synthesized with internal factors in the making of a vocational choice. These factors include race and sex stereotyping, characteristics of occupations, and labor market conditions.

Session 9 helps the participant develop a list of occupations for exploration by focusing on personal interests, aptitudes, experiences, and skills. Extensive research is done on these occupations in Sessions 10 and 11 through the use of the career resources, media, and interviews. This information—plus values and job preferences—serves as the basis for eliminating some occupations and placing the remaining ones in priority order in Session 12. The tentative "first-choice" occupation is used to formulate an "Action Plan" in Session 13; this includes choosing an educational training program and determining the next steps in training and preparation for entry into the occupation. One specific area of implementation skills—job hunting, resume writing, and interviewing—is singled out for special attention in Session 13 before the course wrap-up in Session 14.

Decision Making (Objective 4)

As previously indicated, decision-making skill is viewed as a significant component of vocational maturity (Super, 1974; Crites, 1974; Harren, 1979). Indeed, it is no doubt a significant aspect of maturity in general. Like other skills, decision making can be learned. Although there is little research to provide guidance in the teaching of decision-making skill, it seems evident that the first step is to help individuals to become *aware* of the strategies they are using. An evaluation of these strategies in light of desired outcomes is a prerequisite to altering decision-making behaviors.

There are three topics of particular importance as background material for this session: (1) a model for describing a planful process of deciding, (2) a definition of alternative decision-making styles, and (3) types of decisions to which these styles may be applied. Each of these topics is covered below. If time allows, the leader may choose to enrich this session with some of the additional information.

Planful Decision Making[1]

Since the middle of the century, there has been a great deal of interest in the study of the human phenomenon of decison making. More than twenty models (Smith, 1972) have been proposed to describe this process. Early models emphasized the process as a rational and objective one and attempted to depict it in mathematical terms:

$$\text{Utility of a given alternative} \times \text{Probability of achieving it} = \text{Its value}$$

Later models (Hilton, 1962; Tiedeman & O'Hara, 1963; Tiedeman & Miller, 1972) depicted the process as the finding of the best alternative among those which exist, the one which will most nearly meet the established goal or keep the psychological system in a state of equilibrium for a period of time. Some models (Blau, Parnes, Gustad, Jessor, & Wilcox, 1956) emphasize the pressure of forces outside the individual, while others (Tiedeman & O'Hara, 1963; Tiedeman & Miller, 1972) emphasize the ability of the individual to have primary control over life. Early models tend to define the deciding process as a single straight-line phenomenon, while more recent models emphasize the dynamic and cyclical nature of decision making.

Decison-making models, then, usually are defined in terms of one or more of the following three continua: (1) a purely rational process vs. an intuitive-emotional-rational process, (2) primary control within the individual vs. control outside the individual, and (3) a straight-line, one-time process vs. a cyclical, changing, approximating process. This program recommends and is structured upon the Planful Decision-making Model depicted in Figure 1.

Decision-making Styles

Each individual uses a variety of styles for making or not making decisions. Dinklage (1966) identified and described eight styles which are presented to program participants in this session:

1. *Planful:* Basing a decision on the rational approach, with a balance between the cognitive and the emotional. All seven steps of the process are completed in proper sequence. ("I am planful and organized.")

2. *Agonizing:* Involves much time and thought in gathering data and analyzing alternatives (steps 2-4). The decider gets lost in the pile of information gathered and never gets on to decision point (step 5). ("I can't make up my mind.")

---

[1]The Planful Process is described in *Emphasis Decisions* by Stephen Forrer et al. Copyright 1977 by Olympus Publishing Company, Salt Lake City. Used by permission.

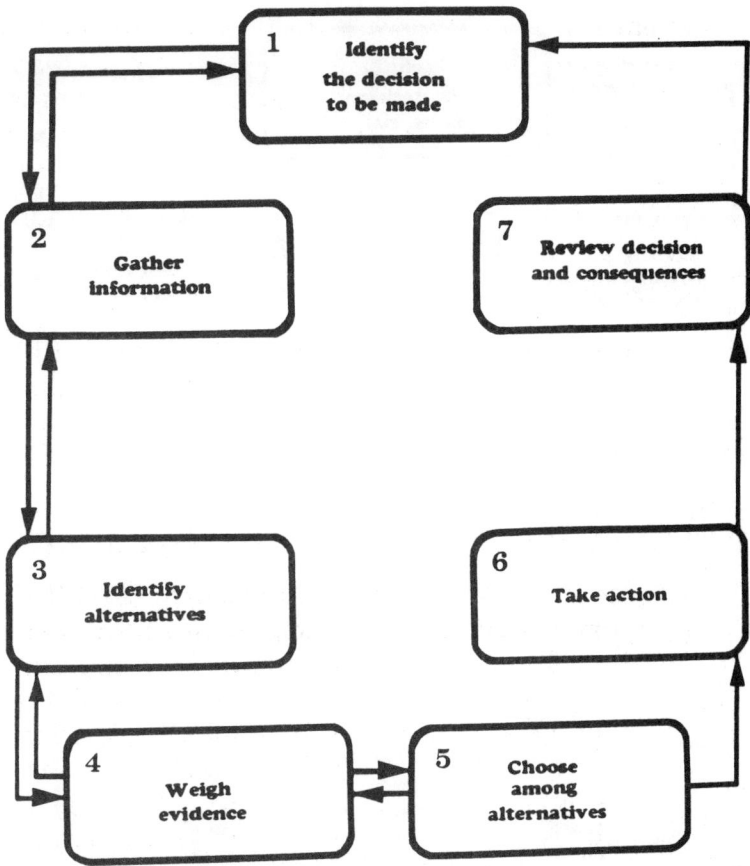

Figure 1. The Planful Decision-making Model.

3. **Impulsive:** Taking the first alternative available, without looking at other alternatives or collecting information. Persons using this strategy move very quickly to step 6. ("Decide now, think later.")

4. **Intuitive:** Basing a decision on feelings which have not been verbalized. ("It feels right.")

5. **Delaying:** Postponing thought and action on a problem until later. ("I'll think about that tomorrow.")

6. **Fatalistic:** Leaving the decision to environment or fate. ("Whatever will be, will be.")

7. **Compliant:** Going along with the plans of someone else rather than making an independent decision. ("If it's OK with you, it's OK with me")

8. **Paralytic:** Accepting the responsibility for a decision but then being unable to set the process in motion to make a decision. ("I know I should, but I just can't get with it.")

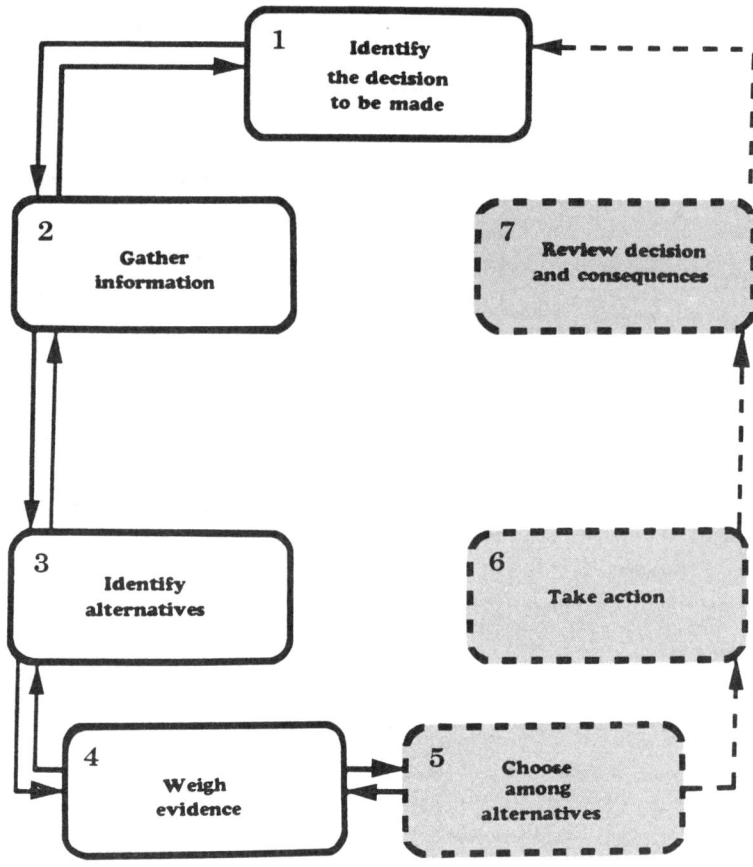

Figure 2. The Impulsive/Intuitive Strategy.

Three of these styles are graphically depicted: the Planful Model (Figure 1), the Impulsive/Intuitive Model (Figure 2), and the Agonizing Model (Figure 3). Steps (from the Planful Model) that are used in these types are outlined in bold, while steps skipped are in dotted outline.

The style of decision making chosen for a given occasion relates to the severity or importance of the possible outcomes and to the type of decision. Using an impulsive strategy for such decisions as the choice of dinner entree or the purchase of a new garment adds spice to life and has relatively short-term and unimportant consequences. An intuitive process is often valuable in selecting friends. However, the use of a planful process is desirable in decisions with heavy consequences, such as buying a house or making a vocational choice. Use of a planful process does not ensure desired outcomes but does increase the probability of them.

Types of Decisions

Life's decisions can be broken into three categories: (1) decisions with certainty, (2) decisions with risk, and (3) decisions with uncertainty. In addition, decisions with risk may

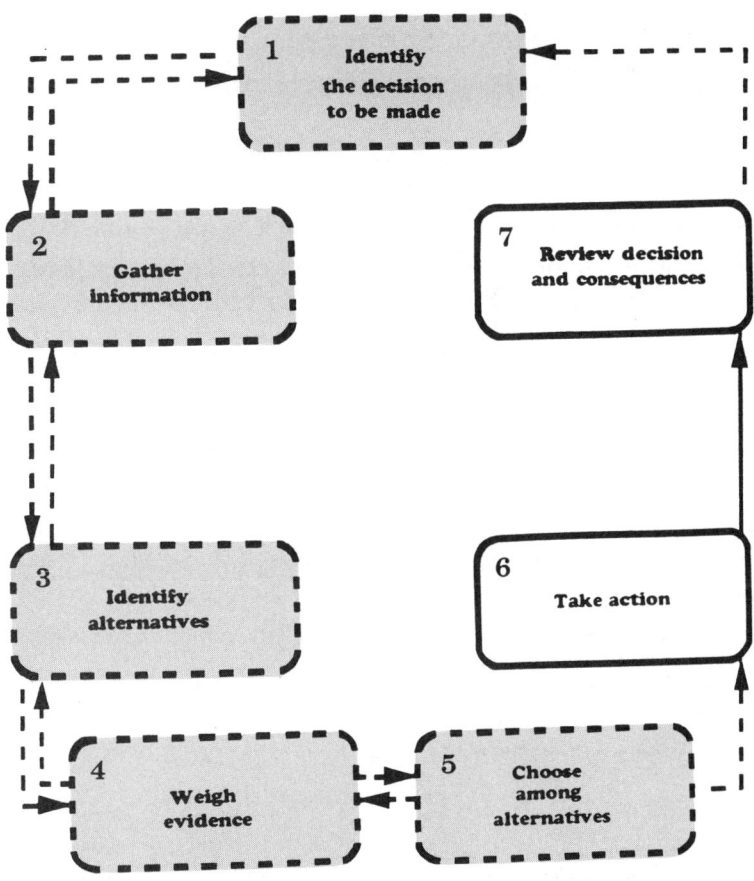

Figure 3. The Agonizing Strategy.

be of two kinds—those with objective probability and those with subjective probability. The three types are defined and illustrated as follows:

1. ***Decisions with certainty.*** These are decisions in which the *outcome* (or consequence) of each alternative *is clearly known.*

    Example: When you get to the stoplight at the bottom of the hill, you can either continue straight or turn left. If you go straight, you will come to the center of town in 1.8 miles. If you turn left, you will leave town and come to Interstate 99 in 4.3 miles.

2. ***Decisions with measured risk.*** These are decisions in which the *outcome* of each alternative *is not totally known, but something is known about the probability* (chances out of 10) or likelihood that a given consequence will occur.

    Examples:

    a. You can attend either of two local colleges: State University or City Community College. If you go to State University, you have six chances out of ten of getting a "C" average or better in your freshman year, based on your ACT scores. If you go to City College, you have eight chances out of ten.

b. Based upon current medical research, if you choose to smoke a pack of cigarettes per day, you double your risk of having a heart attack.

3. ***Decisions with uncertainty.*** These are decisions in which the *outcome* (consequences) of all or some of the alternatives is *totally or almost totally unknown.*

Example: While visiting a strange city, your car breaks down. You know no one to recommend a mechanic and must select one from any listed in the telephone book "Yellow Pages." You have no helpful information about any of them. You can only guess at the outcome.

Although little or no research has been done on this subject, very likely there is a relationship between the type of decision undertaken and the type of strategy selected. In other words, delaying, paralytic, compliant, or fatalistic strategies may be employed much more frequently with decisions of uncertainty. A planful strategy is easier to use with decisions of certainty or decisions of risk with objective probability. An intuitive process may lend itself well to decisions of risk with subjective probabilities.

Although the *Career Planning Guide* does not deal with types of decisions, the leader may find the time or opportunity to introduce this topic.

Session 2
Summary

Objective	Suggested Activities	Suggested Time	Materials
1. To provide a group decision-making experience	Group decision-making exercise (see suggestions on this page).	1 hr.	Selected group decision-making exercise (see options on this page).
2. To identify problems in decision making	Discussion	10-15 min.	None
3. To relate the decision-making process to program content	Mini-lecture	15-20 min.	None

Homework

Read Chapter 3 of the *Career Planning Guide*.

Resource Materials

Group decision-making exercises:

(a) Desert Survival or (b) NASA Moon Survival Task

Objectives and Activities

Objective 1: To provide a group decision-making experience

Suggested activities:

A. Lead the group in one of the following decision-making exercises. These are not a part of this program and should be acquired directly from their respective publishers:

Desert Survival		NASA Moon Survival Task
ELM	or	Teleometrics International
Plymouth, Michigan 48170		P.O. Drawer 1850
		Conroe, Texas 77301

B. Lead the group in discussion of this exercise, utilizing the discussion questions provided with the exercise as well as some like the following:

1. What were some of the most common problems with the group's decision making?

2. What were some of the strengths of the group's decision making?

3. In your opinion, was a better decision reached by group consensus than by individual decision? Why?

4. What inferences drawn from this exercise relate to career decision making?

Possible additional questions:

5. What process was used to arrive at a decision?

6. What issues or questions were considered?

7. What were the differences between the situation analysis, objectives, and alternative courses of action, as identified by the group members? What are the implications in decision making?

8. How were *facts* separated from *assumptions?* What is the difference between these terms, and what are the implications for decision making?

Objective 2: To identify problems in decision making

Suggested activities:

Discussion. The leader introduces the discussion by indicating that some problems in individual and group decision making were identified in the previous group activity. There are additional problems when making decisions. The group is referred to the Planful Strategy schematic and asked to generate ideas about other problems that a decider might experience when trying to follow the steps of this strategy. The leader may list these on the board and should try to elicit at least these kinds of problems:

1. Adequately understanding or expressing the concern which is requiring a decision

2. Making or finding an adequate number of desirable alternatives

3. Finding sufficient and accurate information about alternatives

4. Being able to attach more weight to one or some alternatives in order to begin to focus choice

The leader asks students to volunteer personal experiences with decision making which illustrate each of the types of problems.

Suggested time: 10-15 minutes

Materials: None

Objective 3: To relate decision-making process to program content

Suggested activities:

Mini-lecture. The leader emphasizes that decision making, like other skills, can be learned and sharpened. This concept might be further refined with these ideas:

1. Skills normally go through three stages: (a) learning how to do something (emphasis on cognitive); (b) doing it mechanically at first (emphasis on action); and (c) doing it

with awareness and understanding (emphasis on having incorporated the process into normal behavior patterns).

2. In this program we are attempting to help individuals with Stages 1 and 2. We have completed Stage 1 for the Planful Strategy and will spend a good part of the rest of the time assisting the group to go through Stage 2, using vocational choice as a "practice problem." It is important to learn the skill of decision making because it is critical to the success of total life planning and coping. Emphasis may be placed again on the fact that the Planful Strategy does not ensure good consequences, but it does increase the probability of satisfying consequences.

The leader indicates that from this point on in the program, the Planful Strategy will be applied to the making of a vocational choice, as noted in column 3 of the Syllabus Chart. The leader should also mention at this point, however, that this certainly may not be the "ultimate" vocational choice. Statistics tell us that people change occupations on the average of 4-5 times during their lives, and this number may increase in the future. The purpose here is to learn and use a process which can be used again and again as decisions, especially vocational ones, arise. Since the first step of the Planful Strategy is to define the problem, we will, as a group, define our problem as:

To make a vocational choice.

And we hope all participants will be better equipped to do this by the end of the program. In applying the Planful Strategy to the problem of vocational choice, the second step would be:

To gather information.

Several sessions of the program will assist participants to gather information about themselves and the occupations available to them.

Suggested time: 15-20 minutes

Materials: None

Homework assignment: Read Chapter 3 of the *Career Planning Guide*.

Session 3
Summary

Objective	Suggested Activities	Suggested Time	Materials
1. To apply the concept of the Life-Career Rainbow to personal life and career planning	Definitions of career, occupation, and job	5 min.	None
	Discussion of roles of significant others	10 min.	None
	Complete and discuss Exercise 2, Personal Career Rainbow	15 min.	Exercise 2 of *Career Planning Guide*
2. To relate goals to Career Rainbow roles	Definition of goal	5 min.	None
	Relating goal to Career Rainbow roles and sharing with group	15 min.	Exercise 2 of *Career Planning Guide*
3. To relate self-information to Holland's typology	Mini-lecture on Holland's theory	20 min.	Pages 26-29 of this manual; discussion of Holland types in Chapter 4 of *Career Planning Guide*
	Self-description in a two-letter code	25 min.	

Homework

Read Chapter 4 of the *Career Planning Guide*.

Complete Exercise 3, Vocational Self-Concept Questionnaire.

Begin to read biography or autobiography of at least one famous person.

Supplementary Reading

Super, Donald E., "A Life-Span, Life-Space Approach to Career Development," *Journal of Vocational Behavior*, 1980, *16*, 282-298.

Objectives and Activities

Objective 1: To apply the concept of the Life-Career Rainbow to personal life and career planning

Suggested activities:

A. Ask members of the group to volunteer their definitions of *career, occupation,* and *job.* Provide definitions of these words as given in the *Leader's Manual.* Discuss how the participant's definitions of *career* differ from the one given by Super, studied in today's homework assignment.

B. The leader asks participants to think about adults whom they know. Think particularly about your *mother,* your *father,* an *employer* whom you have had, a *teacher* or *professor,* or a good *friend.*

Think about which roles these people play and how the roles seem to affect their lifestyles and life happiness. Do some of these play too many roles? What effect does that have? Does one, or more than one, play too few roles? What effect does that have? Does one of these spend almost all of his/her time in one role? What effect does that have? Does one or some of these play conflicting roles? The leader asks participants to share information about these individuals in response to these questions.

C. Participants are asked to turn to Exercise 2 in Chapter 3 of the *Career Planning Guide.* Following directions on that sheet, participants are asked to identify roles which they hope to play 10 years from now. Ask participants to share their "careers" today and ten years from now with the group. The leader stimulates discussion with these questions:

1. Which are your primary roles today? Are there any conflicts in these roles?

2. Which roles do you want to be your primary roles ten years from now? Can you foresee any conflicts in those roles?

3. Describe your primary roles ten years from now and the "arenas" in which those roles will be played. What will your work setting and position be like, your home, your children, etc.?

Suggested time: 30 minutes

Materials: Exercise 2 in *Guide*
          Graphic 4—The Life-Career Rainbow

Objective 2: To relate goals to roles on Life-Career Rainbow

Suggested activities:

A. Ask the group to define *goal* and to give some examples of goals. Then ask them to define *short-term goal* and *long-term goal* and give some examples of each.

B. Ask the group to look at Exercise 2 again and to select the three roles which will be of highest importance to them ten years from now. Using the page across from the Life-Career Rainbow exercise sheet, ask individuals to write one long-range goal for each of those primary roles and three short-range goals which relate to each of the three long-range goals.

C. Ask individuals to share their three long-range goals and their short-range goals either in the total group or in small groups.

Suggested time: 20 minutes

Materials: Exercise 2

Objective 3: To relate self-information to Holland's typology

Suggested activities:

A. The leader indicates that one of the most important roles in the Life-Career Rainbow is the role of "worker." To make this a happy and successful role is very much dependent upon understanding the organization of occupations and how to relate oneself to it. Using the background information in Chapter 4, the leader gives a mini-lecture on Holland's (1973) theory. Main points:

1. All individuals can be thought of as a combination of six primary types: Realistic, Investigative, Artistic, Social, Enterprising, and Conventional. The leader describes the characteristics of each of these types of personality.

2. These types develop from a combination of heredity and environment. In general, the types develop according to this pattern:

    a. Certain *activities* and opportunities are provided for children in their early years by the home, school, and community. Parents and significant others reinforce some activities more than others.

    b. Activities that are reinforced become *interests*.

    c. People attempt to develop skill or *competency* in areas in which they have interest.

    d. Having a given set of interests and competencies causes individuals to adopt a related set of *values*.

3. When people of a given "type" work together, they create a unique environment in which they are rewarded for using the interests and competencies they have and for the set of values which they hold.

4. People of a given type attempt to find an environment which is as closely matched to their type as possible.

5. To the extent that people are able to find this match, they have job satisfaction, success on the job, and stability.

B. Based upon the descriptions of the six types that the leader has given (and passed out to the group, if desired), participants are asked to think about themselves and to assign themselves a two-letter "code." The first letter of this code should indicate the one of the six areas in which the individual believes that he or she has highest interest and ability and seems to fit the personality "type." The second letter of this code should indicate a second group in which there is also high interest and ability and a similarity to the personality "type."

C. Participants may be asked to form groups and to tell their self-assigned two-letter code to other members of the group. Each participant explains why he or she believes that this code is appropriate, explaining related interests and abilities. Members of the group may concur with individuals' self-analysis, expand on it, or disagree with it.

Suggested time: 45 minutes

Materials: Section on Holland types in Chapter 4 of *Career Planning Guide*

Homework assignment: Read Chapter 4 of the *Career Planning Guide*.

Complete Exercise 3, Vocational Self-Concept Questionnaire.

Begin to read biography or autobiography of at least one famous person.

Background

Super's Life-Career Rainbow

The following extended excerpt is from Donald E. Super's "How people make and might be helped to make career choices," a paper presented at the CRAC/NICEC Seminar held at King's College, Cambridge, July 1975. It is used by permission.

Life Roles, Theatres, and Styles

Life-stage theory brings out the fact that people play a variety of roles as they mature, and that they play them in a variety of theatres. It is helpful to identify these roles and theatres in order to understand the nature and sequences of careers.

The roles played during the course of a career fall into at least ten categories, as follows:

Life-Career Roles

1. Child
2. Student
3. Worker
4. Spouse
5. Parent
6. Homemaker
7. Citizen
8. "Leisurite"
9. Annuitant
10. Patient

The types of theatres in which they are played are somewhat less numerous, and have been classified as follows:

Life-Career Theatres

1. The Home
2. The Community
3. The School
4. The Workplace
5. The Retirement Community or Home

Roles. These sequential and simultaneous roles may be schematically depicted in the form of an incomplete rainbow, a life-space rainbow which has only one band of color, one role, at each end (infant at the left, nursing home patient at the right), and as many as seven or eight bands or roles at its peak when a person may be pursuing an occupation, maintaining a home, being a spouse, a parent, and the supporting child of an aged parent, engaging in civic work, and indulging his hobbies. In Figure 4 the bands or roles start and stop at different times, as in real life; unlike life roles the life space they occupy is constant in the schematic diagram: in real life, the importance of a given role varies with the life stage.

It should be noted that the occupational role may change several times during a lifetime, or even by a dual role when two simultaneous positions are held: this is why it is incorrect and confusing to use the terms "occupation" and "career" as synonyms, for a career is, both in its etymology and scientific usage, the sequence of positions occupied by a person during his life span, whereas an occupation is a combination of tasks

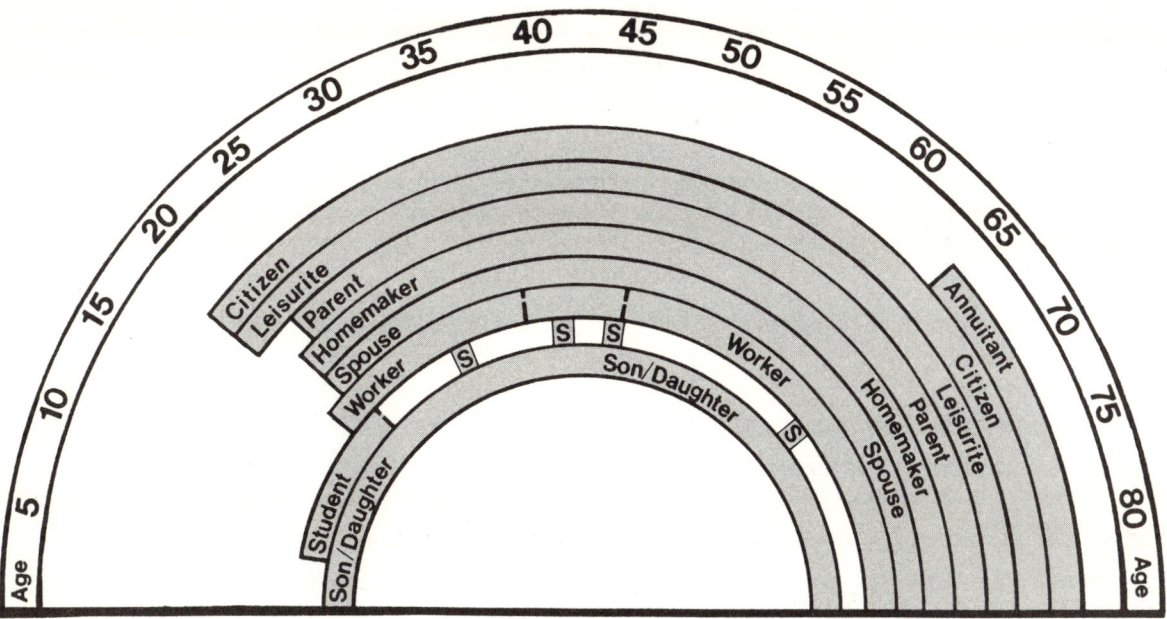

Figure 4. Life-Career Rainbow
(The shaded parts of the rainbow show a career pattern that might be typical for many people.)

performed by people in the production and distribution of goods and services. Any one person may occupy one or more occupational positions at one time, and most occupy several sequentially, during the course of an adult career. The non-occupational positions occupied before and during the adult career influence both the choice of later occupational positions and the ways in which they are occupied; adult position occupancy also determines the post-occupational career through the pattern of retirement activities which it facilitates and through the coping behaviors which the older adult brings to his retirement role expectations, positions, and tasks.

The more adequately the adolescent plays his pre-occupational roles, the more success and satisfaction he will have in playing his adult roles. This is shown by the substantial correlations between secondary school grades, extracurricular activities, and participation in community organizations and activities while in school, on the one hand, and both occupational and career satisfaction at age 25 and at age 36 in the Career Pattern Study (Super, Kowalski & Gotkin, 1967; Jordaan & Super, 1974). As Havighurst (1953, 1962), hypothesized, coping with the developmental tasks of one life stage is basic to coping with those of the next life stage.

The greater the number of simultaneous roles the individual successfully plays at one life stage, the richer his life style, and the greater also his likelihood of playing a variety of later roles successfully and with satisfaction. Furthermore, the greater the number of roles played simultaneously in adulthood (within the limits set by clock, calendar, and capacities) the greater the degree of self-actualization and of satisfaction. And, as Steer (1970) has shown, the greater also the likelihood of finding satisfying roles in retirement.

The fact that, willy-nilly, people play several roles simultaneously, in several theatres, means that occupation, family, community, and leisure have impact on each other. Success in one facilitates success in another, and difficulties in one are likely to lead to difficulties in others. This principle is well illustrated by the case of John Stasko (Super, 1957), whose marriage with a woman better educated than he aggravated his feelings of inferiority and upset his health, and whose successful coping with his occupational problems, facilitated by vocational counseling, led to better familial adjustment and to better health.

Theatres. Careers are indeed complex phenomena. At their peak, each role is played to some degree in several theatres, as when a working mother must respond to an emergency call about a sick child or a husband and father takes work home at nights and devotes less time than his wife and children think he should to familial and homemaking concerns such as talking with his wife, playing with the children, and repairing broken furniture and toys. Similarly, each theatre chosen is to some extent determined by the roles one plays, as when a young lawyer is active in civic affairs because it helps to promote his occupational career, and when a young mother joins a parents' association to play a civic role in order to help her children and to enrich her own life.

Life Styles. It is this combination of waxing and waning roles, of utilized and abandoned theatres, that structures life. It has frequently been found (Friedman & Havighurst, 1954; Super, 1957; O'Toole et al., 1973) that work structures life and gives it meaning, providing a schedule according to which life is lived, associates who supply social support, and content which gives it meaning. Occupation thus sets the life style, just as the life style leads to entry into an occupation. The several life roles are reciprocal forces in shaping careers.

Definitions of key terms in Session 3

Career—the sum total of life roles, including the Worker role, that an individual is playing at a given time

Occupation—a definable set of work activities that members of an occupational group engage in

Job—a group of similar positions in a business, industry, or other place of employment

Brief Overview of the Theory and Work of John Holland

For complete understanding, read *Making Vocational Choices: A Theory of Careers* by John L. Holland (Englewood Cliffs, New Jersey: Prentice-Hall, 1973).

  I. Some basic assumptions

  A. The choice of an occupation is an expression of personality. Vocational interests are the expression of personality in work, hobbies, recreational activities, and preferences.

  B. Interest inventories are personality inventories.

  C. Occupational stereotypes have reliable and important psychological meanings.

  D. The members of an occupational group have similar personalities and similar histories of personal development.

  E. Because people in an occupational group have similar personalities, they will respond to many situations and problems in similar ways; thus, they create characteristic interpersonal environments.

  F. Vocational satisfaction, stability, and achievement depend upon the congruency between one's personality and the environment in which one works.

  II. The theory

  A. Most persons can be categorized as one of six types: Realistic, Investigative,

Artistic, Social, Enterprising, or Conventional. These six types are described on pages 28-29.

1. These types result from the interaction between a particular heredity and a variety of cultural and personal forces. The pattern of development proceeds as follows:

    a. Certain *activities* performed by children are reinforced by their parents and other significant adults.

    b. These reinforced activities become *interests*.

    c. Individuals develop *competencies* in areas of their interest.

    d. Having and using a set of competencies leads to holding a unique set of *values*.

2. Individuals seek their own educational level (often equals prestige) within types based upon ability and motivation.

B. As individuals of a given type work together, they create a unique environment; thus, there are also six types of environments.

C. Individuals search for occupations and environments that will permit them to use their skills and abilities, express their attitudes and values, and be rewarded for them.

D. An individual's behavior, vocational success, vocational stability, and vocational satisfaction can be explained by the interaction of his or her personality pattern and work environment.

III. Some interesting research findings

A. The world of occupations can be viewed in six or more groups, contiguously arranged in a circular configuration (see World-of-Work Map, page 36 of this manual).

1. This is highly consistent with Roe's earlier eight-category classification system (Ann Roe, *Psychology of Occupations*, New York: John Wiley and Sons, 1956).

2. These six groups can also be viewed from the perspective of the relationship of the work tasks to an ideas, data, people, and things orientation (see World-of-Work Map).

B. These six groups form a hexagonal model (Figure 5), and the six points on the hexagon have an empirically-tested relationship to each other (see correlation coefficients in hexagon). The relationships among the six Holland occupational categories can be interpreted by using the hexagonal model. The main categories are arranged in clockwise order: R, I, A, S, E, C. Interrelationships of occupations from the hexagon should be interpreted as follows. *Adjacent categories* are most *alike*—for example, Social and Enterprising occupations. *Opposites* on the hexagon are most *unlike*—for example, Conventional and Artistic. The categories at intermediate distances (e.g., Social and Investigative) are somewhat unlike.

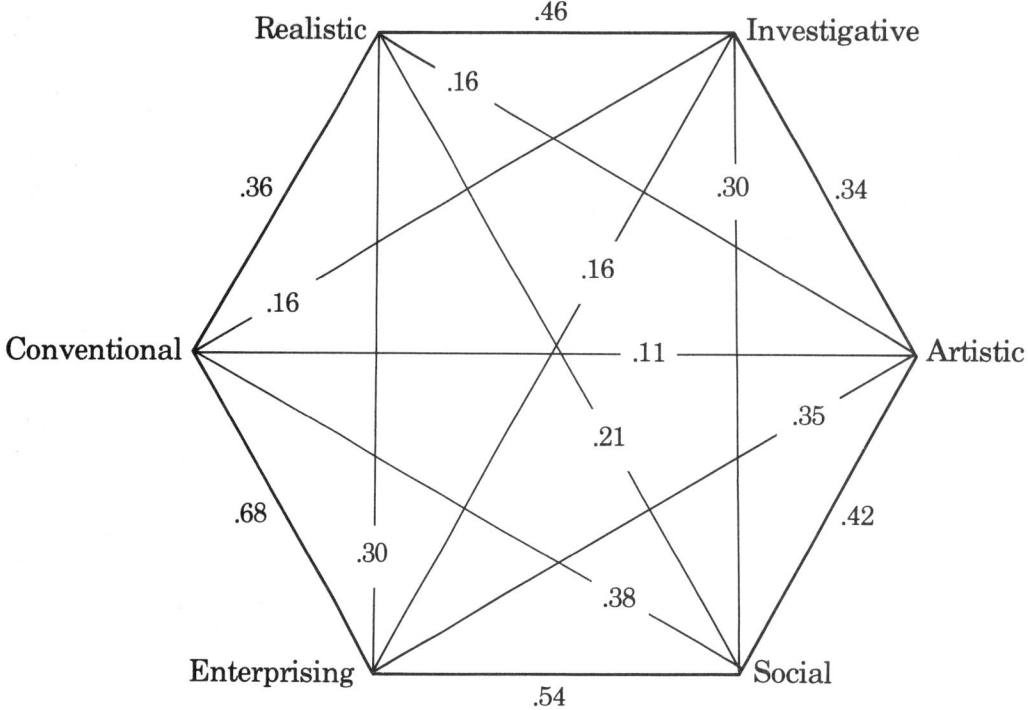

Figure 5. A Hexagonal Model for Interpreting Relationships of the Holland Occupational Categories.

(Source: J. L. Holland, D. R. Whitney, N. S. Cole, and J. M. Richards, Jr. *An empirical occupational classification derived from a theory of personality and intended for practice and research,* ACT Research Report No. 29, Iowa City, Iowa: The American College Testing Program, 1969.)

Explanation of the Six Holland Types

People of the **Realistic** type

- like to work with tools, objects, machines, or animals.
- develop manual, mechanical, agricultural, and electrical skills.
- prefer jobs in which they can build or repair things.
- are usually down-to-earth people.

People of the **Investigative** type

- like activities that lead to learning more about the biological and physical sciences.
- develop very good ability in math and science.
- prefer jobs in scientific and medical fields.
- are described as curious, studious, and independent.

People of the **Artistic** type

- like to feel free from scheduled routine so that time can be used for creative activities.
- develop skills in language, art, music, drama, and writing.
- prefer jobs in which they can use their talent for creative writing.

People of the **Social** type

- like activities that involve informing, training, teaching, understanding, and helping others.
- develop ability to work with people.
- prefer occupations such as teaching, nursing, and counseling.
- like to be thought of as helpful and friendly.

People of the **Enterprising** type

- like activities that permit leading or influencing other people.
- develop leadership ability and persuasive and other important skills in relating to people.
- prefer jobs such as salesperson or manager.
- are ambitious, outgoing, energetic, and self-confident.

People of the **Conventional** type

- like activities that permit organization of information in a clear and orderly way.
- develop office and arithmetical skills.
- prefer jobs like preparing records, filing papers, typing letters, and operating computers.
- like to be thought of as responsible and dependable.

Session 4
Summary

Objectives	Suggested Activities	Suggested Time	Materials
1. To discuss the self-concept	Mini-lecture and class discussion	15-20 min.	None
2. To make the relationship between self-concept and roles of the Life-Career Rainbow	Mini-lecture	10-15 min.	Graphic 4—The Life-Career Rainbow
	Exercise 3, Vocational Self-Concept Questionnaire	10-15 min.	Exercise 3 of *Career Planning Guide*
3. To introduce concept of the World-of-Work Map	Mini-lecture	15 min.	Pages 36-43 of this manual

Homework

Read Chapter 5 of the *Career Planning Guide*.

Complete Exercise 4A.

Continue reading biography or autobiography and write report (due in Session 5).

Supplementary Reading

Super, Donald E. et al. *Career Development: Self-Concept Theory*. Princeton, N.J.: College Entrance Examination Board, 1963.

Resource Material

Work and You. Barr Films, 3490 E. Foothill Boulevard, Pasadena, Calif. 91107 (1976). A 16mm. film which explores reasons people must work, and explores alternatives within the areas related to an individual's interests, abilities, and potentials.

Objectives and Activities

Objective 1: To discuss the self-concept

Suggested activities:

A. *Mini-lecture on self-concept:*

Utilizing the background material provided here and additional reading or knowledge. the leader provides a mini-lecture on the self-concept, its formation, and its implementation in life roles, including the worker role.

Suggested time: 15-20 minutes

Materials: None

B. The leader stimulates group discussion related to their reading and the mini-lecture. Suggested discussion questions:

1. Suppose an individual has a very undefined or "poor" self-concept. How is this likely to affect his or her vocational choice? (May have difficulty making choice or may make an unwise choice.)

2. Suppose an individual is confined to an occupation that doesn't "fulfill" the self-concept because of inadequate training/education or the demands of the job market. What implications might this have for the individual's life? (The need to fulfill self-concept in other roles of the Life-Career Rainbow and/or the acquisition of new skills or education.)

3. Think about your family and friends. Can you give examples of individuals in which occupation really does implement the self-concept and examples where occupation definitely does not?

4. As you thought about your life while doing the assignment exercise in the *Career Planning Guide,*

   a. What effects did you note on the development of your own self-concept?

   b. Are there ways to modify these effects if they have not been positive? How?

   c. Assuming that self-concept has a strong effect upon vocational and other choices, what would you want to do as a parent (or other "significant" adult) to make this effect as positive as possible?

   d. Do you expect that your self-concept will change over time? Why? What might that mean for future vocational choice?

Suggested time: 15-20 minutes

Materials: None

Objective 2: To relate self-concept to roles of the Life-Career Rainbow

Suggested activities:

A. Mini-lecture

The leader calls attention again to the Life-Career Rainbow (Figure 3.1). This may be done by asking the group to turn to the rainbow in the *Career Planning Guide* or by using the Life-Career Rainbow graphic again. The central focus of this mini-lecture is that we self-actualize (i.e., fulfill our self-concepts) through *all* the roles of the Career Rainbow and to a large extent we can choose how to implement self-concept across the roles.

Events which occur in some roles cause a change in the level of fulfillment needed in other roles. Losing a spouse, for example, may cause an individual to need or expect greater life fulfillment from the Worker role. Having a very fulfilling Worker role may cause an individual to eliminate the Citizen role (or even the Parent role) or to reduce drastically the time and energy spent in the Homemaker role.

Suggested time: 10-15 minutes

Materials: Career Rainbow graphic

B. Vocational Self-Concept Questionnaire (Exercise 3)

Participants are asked to form groups of 5-6 participants and to share the content of the Vocational Self-Concept Questionnaire with each other. The leader may process this exercise by asking groups to report some general inferences from this exercise.

Suggested time: 10-15 minutes

Materials: Pages 32-34 of *Career Planning Guide*

C. Optional exercise to relate self-concept to occupations (Worker role)

The leader divides participants into six groups and gives each group a description of one occupation. These descriptions can either be copied onto cards from pages 44-48 of this manual, or pages can be duplicated and cut into strips. An appointed group leader within each group should read the occupational description to the members and should lead a discussion about the type of person (in terms of self-concept, personality, characteristics, interests, values, abilities, etc.) who would probably enjoy this job. After each of the six groups has finished discussion, the leader asks each group leader to read the occupational description to the total group and then to summarize the discussion of the small group. Since each group is dealing with a stereotypical occupation in each of Holland's six groups (studied in Session 3), the instructor can use the group reports as a summary of Holland's classification system and to point out how different types of personalities (i.e., self-concepts) can be "implemented" in occupations. This exercise can be repeated a second time with six different occupations if time allows.

Suggested time: 10-20 minutes

Materials: Description of 12 Occupations, **pages 44-48 of this manual**

Homework assignment: Read Chapter 5 of the *Career Planning Guide*.

    Complete Exercise 4A.

    Continue reading a biography or autobiography of a famous person in any occupation.

    Prepare to write a 5-6 page report on your biography or autobiography. In this report you are to:

    a. Describe the self-concept of the person and how this was developed, strengthened, and/or diminished;

    b. Describe the interests, skills (talents, abilities), and experiences of the person and how these were developed, reinforced, or extinguished; and

    c. Explain the implications of a and b for selection of roles on the Life-Career Rainbow, especially of the occupation in the Worker role; and of your evaluation of the person's life in terms of "good" or "poor" implementation of self-concept.

Background

Self-Concept and Vocational Choice

The first three sessions of the Life and Career Planning Program have attempted to provide some general background information about the dimensions of career and of the World of Work. The program now turns to a detailed collection of self-information—that is, an examination of the internal factors which affect vocational choice and development. Among these internal factors are interests, aptitudes/skills, values, and goals. These factors interact with each other to constitute a significant part of the self-concept.

Self-concept might be defined simply as the picture one holds of oneself. Both career development and vocational choice theorists recognize the central importance of the self-concept in the making of a vocational choice. Super (1963) maintains that the choice of an occupation is the implementation of a self-concept. Holland (1973) develops a very similar theme when he states that the special heredity and early environment of a child lead to a preference for certain types of *activities*. Those activities which are reinforced by parents and significant others become *interests*. Still later, these interests lead to the development of *competencies* and the adoption of a set of related *values*. All these factors combine to create a given personality type and self-concept.

Super (1963) has developed a detailed theory of the self-concept and its relationship to vocational choice. As soon as infants begin to recognize that they are separate entities from parents, toys, or objects of furniture, the self-concept has begun to form. The process of development, differentiation, and integration of the self-concept continues throughout life and is never, therefore, "finished" or static. Especially through childhood and adolescence, individuals develop "self-snapshots" of how they are in a variety of different situations: as students, as children, as friends, as players of different games and sports. These many, and perhaps quite different, self-concepts are integrated into a *self-concept system*. The parts of the self-concept system that are transferable to the worker life role can be called the *vocational self-concept*. This set of self-pictures and statements most heavily influences vocational choice.

Super and other theorists generally agree that the self-concept is composed essentially of three parts: (1) the way we see ourselves, (2) the way we think others see us, and (3) the way we would ideally like to be. Obviously, the greater the overlap among these three, the greater the integration of the person. Especially the first two components of the self-concept—how we see ourselves and how we think others see us—are significantly affected by the patterns of positive and negative reinforcement received. The primary sources of this reinforcement are the home, the peer group, and the school.

Super contends that the self-concept cannot be measured or assessed by instruments or techniques external to the individual. The self-concept must be the set of statements which the individual is able to verbalize about self. The self-concept exercises in this session are designed to stimulate such self-statements. These statements can be characterized according to a number of "metadimensions" (Super, 1963):

Self-esteem—the degree to which the view of the self is positive;

Clarity—the degree of awareness exhibited in the self-concept;

Abstraction—the ability to describe self in general terms rather than only in concrete and specific terms;

Refinement—the degree to which traits ascribed to self can be elaborated;

Certainty—the degree of confidence a person has about the traits ascribed to self;

Stability—the degree of consistency of the self-description over time; and

Realism—the degree of agreement between the individual's picture of self and external, objective evidence.

As facilitator you may want to listen to participant self-statements in Session 4 with these metadimensions in mind. To the extent that individuals have a significant degree of each of these metadimensions, the self-concept may be ready for implementation in a vocational choice.

Super's work on life roles (1980) opens an even larger arena for the implementation of self-concepts. Obviously, self-concept is implemented in all of the roles one assumes in "career." This means that some interests, skills, and values may be implemented in nonworker roles because the individual chooses to have it this way; or lack of training, skills, or jobs dictates it. The individual may choose to apply the skill "good at working with my hands" in the Leisurite role instead of the Worker role. The ability to help others may be put to use in the Citizen role or Parent role instead of the Worker role. Prestige or leadership may be a part of the Citizen role instead of the Worker role. Likewise, changing life events may influence the selection and augmentation of roles. Divorce or children leaving the home may cause an individual to seek greater self-fulfillment in other life roles. These same events may prompt the addition of the roles of Student or Worker. Thus, it is imperative to consider self-concept fulfillment as a dynamic function that cuts across all life roles.

Tiedeman (1963) describes the process of career development as an ongoing chain of differentiation and integration. Differentiation refers to an ever-increasing ability to perceive shades of difference, either in the self or in the environment of which the self is a part. The increasing awareness of differentiation of the self and of the environment leads to a state of integration of the two, which in turn facilitates vocational choice. Career development is a continued refinement of this process.

Holland's explanation (1973) of the development of a personality type is similar to Tiedeman's. Holland proposes that each individual is a combination of two or more of his six types, described earlier in this manual. Becoming a given type predisposes an individual to seek occupational environments in which his or her competencies can be utilized, interests fulfilled, and value system rewarded. This process reinforces Super's view that the choice of an occupation is the implementation of a self-concept.

These theorists provide the theoretical background for our attention to the self-concept. It is obvious that an unclear self-picture cannot be easily "translated" into vocational alternatives. The central purpose of Session 4 is to develop in the participants clear self-concepts, which can then be effectively applied to vocational planning as the Life and Career Planning Program progresses.

The World-of-Work Map

The sessions following this one are designed to assist individuals to identify elements of the self-concept—interests, skills, experiences, and abilities—and to relate these to occupations. The construct for accomplishing this is the World-of-Work Map, a refinement of Holland's hexagonal model. The following article describes the development, meaning, and utility of this organizational structure. It provides the background needed for the mini-lecture and for understanding the instruments and procedures in subsequent sessions. Figure 6 provides the link between the six Holland groups and the World-of-Work Map, developed by The American College Testing Program.

Figure 6. The World-of-Work Map for Job Families with Holland groups. Copyright 1974 by The American College Testing Program.

A World-of-Work Map for Career Exploration[2]

Dale J. Prediger

This article briefly describes the development, characteristics, and use of the World-of-Work Map and the associated American College Testing Program Occupational Classification System (ACT-OCS). The main purpose of the map and ACT-OCS is to provide persons at an early stage of career planning with an overview of the world of work and to help them identify personally relevant occupational options.

Rationale for the Map and ACT-OCS

Those who seek to provide help with career exploration and planning have long recognized the need to organize and summarize the complex world of work; as a result, a number of occupational classification systems have been developed. These systems range from the 15 industry-based clusters developed by the U.S. Office of Education (USOE) [14] to the 72-group, psychologically based typology constructed by Holland [8]. Undoubtedly, the most widely used and influential occupational classification systems are those appearing in the *Dictionary of Occupational Titles* (DOT) [12].

A review of these systems and more than 15 others identified in a search of the professional literature indicated that, from the standpoint of career guidance, each has certain strengths and weaknesses. Because of the complexity of work, each system makes certain compromises to achieve its desired emphases. Classification systems that provide a comprehensive overview of the work world (e.g., the DOT occupational group arrangement and the USOE clusters) cannot easily be used to help persons identify career options appropriate to their characteristics. On the other hand, systems intended to help persons relate their characteristics to occupations (e.g., the DOT worker trait groups and Holland's 3-letter code system for personality types) usually group occupations on the basis of human traits rather than the nature of the work. Often the groups are numerous.

As indicated by the following guidelines, a proper balance between these two emphases was sought in developing the ACT-OCS and World-of-Work Map. They must (a) encompass the entire world of work; (b) apply to persons at various stages of career exploration and planning; (c) provide an overview of the world of work in occupational terms (group occupations on the basis of similarities in duties, purpose of work, and work settings rather than by industry or by the psychological traits of workers); and (d) help persons identify occupations for exploration on the basis of their educational plans and personal characteristics, their interests, and abilities.

Overview of the Classification System

To accomplish the first objective all occupations listed in the DOT were used as primary units of analysis in developing the classification system. To achieve the second objective a hierarchical classification system was developed. At the most general level of the hierarchy, persons are introduced to 6 job clusters similar in nature to the occupational groups developed by Roe [10] and Holland [8]. The job cluster titles are shown in Figure 7. At the second level, 25 job families are used to summarize the complexity of the work world. Examples include medicine and medical technologies; retail sales and services; creative arts; and machine operating, servicing, and repairing. Since the 25 job families are organized by job clusters, with an average of 4 per cluster, their number is not unmanageable. (The work *job* is used in job cluster because the classification system is intended for use with students; *occupation* would be more appropriate for a professional audience.)

At the third level of the hierarchy each job family is subdivided into 3 categories according to the formal job preparation required. Finally, *650 occupational titles* are listed according to cluster, family, and type of preparation. In some cases the job titles comprise a range of individual occupations (e.g., retail sales workers, elementary school teachers). The list of 25 job families and 650 job titles is available at no cost from the author.

As an alternative classification procedure, the ACT-OCS provides for the division of the 25 job families into the 603 3-digit occupational code groups used in the DOT. The job families have also been cross-referenced [1] to

---

[2]Originally appeared in *Vocational Guidance Quarterly*, 1976, 24, 198-208. Reprinted by permission.

Dale J. Prediger is Director, Developmental Research Department, The American College Testing Program, Iowa City, Iowa.

DOT worker trait groups, the *Occupational Outlook Handbook* [13]. the USOE Career Clusters, 3 commercially available files of occupational descriptions, and high school courses. Job clusters are cross-referenced to career guidance activities, units, and audio-visual aids.

In summary, the ACT-OCS groups occupations according to job cluster, job family, and type of preparation. Because only 25 job families are involved and because each has been subdivided into the same job preparation categories, specificity is obtained without sacrificing simplicity, and users can choose the level of specificity desired.

Summary of Development

The third and fourth objectives for the ACT-OCS appear, at first glance, to be incompatible. The classification system must provide an overview of the work world in occupational terms, and, at the same time, it must have a psychological basis to help students relate their personal charateristics to occupations. The identification of basic work task dimensions characterizing both occupations and people's activity preferences provided the link for the third and fourth objectives.

Basic Work Task Dimensions. Currently, two well-known and highly similar occupational classification systems [8; 11] allocate occupations to six and eight broad groups respectively and arrange these groups in a circular order to show similarities and differences. Roe's classification system groups occupations and arranges them according to "primary focus of activity" [10, p. 144], whereas Holland's system is psychologically based. Roe acknowledges the similarity between activity focus and basic types of human interests.

According to Roe and Holland, adjacent groups in their circular ordering of occupations are most similar and groups on opposite sides of the circle are least similar. A circle, of course, is two-dimensional, thus suggesting that there are two basic dimensions on which occupations differ. Although Roe [10] and, more recently, Roe and Klos [11] speculated on the nature of these dimensions, no attention has been given to this question in Holland's theory or occupational classification system [8]. Figure 7 shows the general configuration of the Roe and Holland occupational clusters and related clusters in the ACT-OCS. The two work task dimensions—data/ideas and people/things—suggested by the arrangement of the job clusters are also shown. Both dimensions are compatible with the dimensions proposed by Roe and Klos [11].

Although the people/things dimension has been widely recognized in the literature on interest measurement, the possibility of a data/ideas work task dimension has received relatively little attention. Indeed, the DOT "data-people-things" ratings combine data and ideas work tasks into one category. Research on the viability of the two work task dimensions suggested by the Roe and Holland classification systems is briefly summarized here.

Analyses of DOT data. Information on the characteristics of each of the 13,800 occupations identified as unique in the DOT was obtained on computer tape from the U.S. Department of Labor. This information (data-people-things codes, interest ratings, temperament ratings, work field/activity codes) was combined and summarized into data, ideas, people, and things scores for each occupation. The correlation between the data and ideas scores was -.67, which happened to be the same correlation found between the people and things scores. However, correlations for other combinations of the four scores (e.g., things and ideas) ranged around zero (-.29 to .27). These results indicated two bipolar dimensions: a data/ideas dimension and a people/things dimension. Occupations having high involvement with data as a primary work task, such as accounting, tended to have relatively low involvement with ideas. Conversely, occupations having high involvement with ideas, such as creative writing, tended to have low involvement with data. Occupations with high people involvement tended to have low things involvement, and vice versa.

When data/ideas and people/things dimensions were formed from the four separate scores, a correlation of .27 was found for the two dimensions. This correlation indicates that the two work task dimensions are relatively independent.

Analyses of occupational group data. The same work task dimensions found in the DOT data were also found in an analysis of the interest profiles for occupational groups on the basic scales of the Strong Vocational Interest Blank [2], the Project TALENT interest scales [6], and Holland's Vocational Preference Inventory [9]. In a principal components analysis of each of these three sets of data, the two work task dimensions were the main dimensions of interests assessed by the measures. That is, the occupations in the analyses differed most

Figure 7. Relationship Between Job Clusters and the Data/Ideas, People/Things Work Task Dimensions

Note: Roe and Holland job cluster titles related to ACT-OCS titles are shown in parentheses. Roe titles appear first.

on these two dimensions. Furthermore, the occupations distributed themselves on the two dimensions in sensible ways. For example, high school English teachers scored toward the people and ideas poles of the two dimensions, whereas business education teachers scored toward the people and data poles. Over 500 occupational groups with a total membership of approximately 100,000 persons were involved in these analyses.

Definitions of Work Tasks. Archetypal definitions of the poles of the two bipolar work task dimensions are provided below, with alternate terms appearing in parentheses.

Data (facts, records, files, numbers; systematic procedures for facilitating goods/services consumption by people). Data tasks involve *impersonal processes,* such as recording, verifying, transmitting, and organizing facts or data representing goods and services. Purchasing agents, accountants, and air traffic controllers work mainly with data.

Ideas (abstractions, theories, knowledge, insights, and new ways of expressing something, for example, with words, equations, or music). Ideas tasks involve *intrapersonal processes,* such as creating, discovering, interpreting, and synthesizing abstractions or implementing applications of abstractions. Scientists, musicians, and philosophers work mainly with ideas.

People. People tasks involve *interpersonal processes,* such as helping, informing, serving, persuading, entertaining, motivating, and directing—in general, producing a change in human behavior. Teachers, salespersons, and nurses work mainly with people.

Things (machines, mechanisms, materials, tools, physical and biological processes). Things tasks involve *nonpersonal processes,* such as producing, transporting, servicing, and repairing. Bricklayers, farmers, and engineers work mainly with things.

All occupations have some involvement with data, ideas, people, and things; the examples above were chosen with emphasis on the primary purpose or focus of the job tasks [10]. For example, scientists may work with data but their primary purpose is not to produce or handle data; rather, it is to create or apply scientific knowledge. Likewise, an accountant may work with ideas but the ultimate goal is not to create ideas; it is to organize, record, and verify data in a systematic manner.

Formation of Job Families. Through successive revisions, occupations in the DOT were allocated to job families relatively homogeneous with respect to involvement with data/ideas and people/things. At the same time, care was taken to ensure that the job families made sense in terms of the types of occupations grouped together. Initially, 30 job families were formed and each was assigned to one of the 6 clusters. These job families were tried out in May 1972 with 1,600 9th-grade students in 6 schools, to determine the difficulties students had in understanding and using the classification system.

Information from these tryouts and new analyses of DOT worker trait ratings led to further revisions in the system. A version containing 25 job families was used with approximately 32,000 students in the spring 1973 norming of ACT's Career Planning Program, Grades 8-11 [1]. One of the exercises in the Career Planning Program asks students to report their first occupational preference and then assign it to a job family. Accuracy of assignment was studied for a random sample of 400 8th- and 11th-grade students in 40 schools [1]. Approximately 85 percent of both grade groups classified their occupational preferences into the appropriate job families; students who made incorrect classifications usually identified a job family closely associated with the appropriate one.

Information from the norm group study, along with the theoretical considerations and research results cited here, led to further revisions of the classifiction system. Also considered were the locations of the DOT 3-digit occupational groups on Holland's circular arrangement, as determined from Holland's interest profile codes for each of the 603 groups [8]. The current job family structure synthesizes and summarizes information from all these resources. Allocation of occupations to the three job preparation categories was based on DOT ratings for the amount of time involved in preparing for the occupations, supplemented by information in the *Occupational Outlook Handbook* [13].

Location of Job Families on Map. Job families are located on the World-of-Work Map (Figure 8) according to the relative standing of their member occupations on the two work task dimensions. The same data used in allocating occupations to job families (DOT ratings, occupational group profiles on the three interest inventories mentioned previously, and Holland's codes for DOT groups) were synthesized in determining typical involvement with data/ideas and people/things work tasks. Although care was taken to make job familes as homogeneous as possible on the two work task dimensions, there is still considerable scatter among the occupations in a job family. Arrows on the map indicate the nature of this scatter when it is unusually large.

It should be emphasized that the World-of-Work Map summarizes information for approximately 13,800 occupations; it is application oriented and is not meant to constitute a precise scientific statement. ACT hopes and intends that the map and the classification system on which it is based will be the subject of continued study, revision, and improvement.

Placing Persons on the Map. Research indicates that the work task dimensions found for occupations can also be used to summarize the work task preferences of general samples of people. For example, the same two work task dimension described earlier were found in analyses of the interest scores of large, nationwide samples of 8th-, 9th-, and 11th-grade students [1], and college-bound 12th grade students [7]. As noted earlier, Roe [10] recognized the similarity between the "primary focus of activity" used in forming her occupational classification system and the basic types of vocational interests. Indeed, a factor analysis of four interest and personality inventories completed by Cottle [4] more than 25 years ago suggested similar bipolar dimensions of work task preferences.

Thus, there are common dimensions for comparing job-related activity preferences with the work tasks characterizing the 25 job families. That is, job-related activity preferences can be transformed to positions on the data/ideas and people/things dimensions, and this information can be used to plot a person's location among the job families on the World-of-Work Map. However, for purposes of career exploration, only a general region need be indicted to a counselee. Accordingly, the World-of-Work Map was arbitrarily divided into the 13 regions shown in Figure 2. Twelve of the regions, each covering 30° on the map, span the world of work. The 13th region ("region 99") is used to indicate undifferentiated work task preferences (a "flat" profile).

Using the Map

The occupational classification system and map shown in miniature in Figure 8 and the materials associated with them provide an overview of the world of work, the main purpose of the ACT-OCS and map. (A larger reproduction of the map, which can be used in career counseling, is available at no cost from the author.) Informal and formal procedures for accomplishing the other purpose of the World-of-Work Map—helping counselees identify personally relevant occupational options—are briefly described in the following pages.

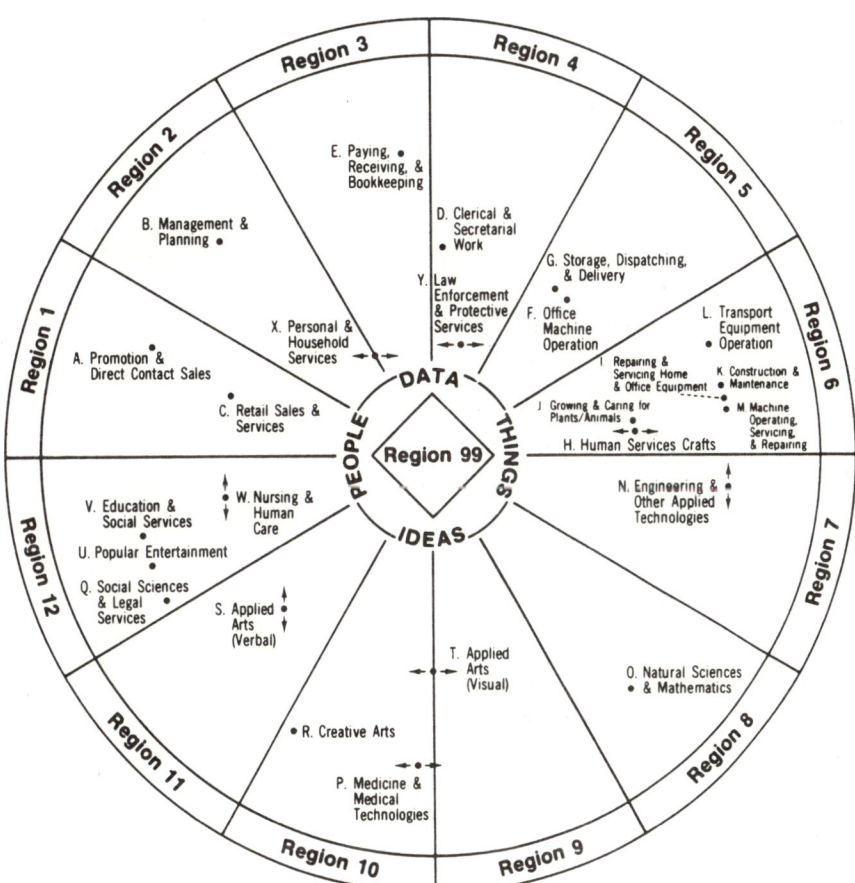

Figure 8. World-of-Work Map.

Note: Map locates job families according to primary involvement with data, ideas, people, and things. Arrows by a job family show that work tasks often heavily involve both people and things (← →) or data and ideas (↑ ↓). The following two job families are not on the map: personal and household services, and law enforcement and protective services. Occupations in these families tend to fall in the inner area of Regions 2 through 5, indicating a generally low involvement with data and people or things, depending on the occupation.

41

Informal Procedures. One procedure for placing persons on the map starts with their current occupational preferences. For example, the job family appropriate to a student's first occupational preference can be identified and its location found on the World-of-Work Map. This location determines the student's region, which, in turn, provides a tentative description of the student's work task preferences. Usually students will not have thought of occupations or their own activity preferences in terms of basic work tasks. Neither will they have considered other occupations in their job family or the families nearby. Thus, a single occupational preference can be used to suggest a wide range of occupational options and to initiate discussion of information about self.

An alternative procedure for placing persons on the map begins with work task preferences. For example, student-oriented descriptions of the four basic work tasks can be incorporated into group discussions of the varieties of work and associated life styles. Self-ratings of preferences for working with data, ideas, people, and things can then be collected and used to find appropriate regions on the map. Region 12 might be suggested to someone whose preference is to work first with people and second with ideas (see Figure 8). Regions 6 and 7 might be explored by someone who prefers to work with things and expresses no preference between data and ideas. Once a region on the map has been determined, by whatever means, counselors can help students identify and explore job families in and around the region. The list of occupations by job family will be useful in this activity.

These counseling procedures expand career exploration and, at the same time, provide focus. Counselors should point out, however, that a student's region on the map is only approximate and is subject to change as interests change. Students should also be informed of the map's limitations noted previously. Finally, students should recognize that work task preferences only provide a starting point for career exploration. Many other things, personal and environmental, must be considered.

Formal Procedures. The general correspondence between scales on five frequently used interest inventories and the data, ideas, people, and things poles of the two work task dimensions is summarized in Table 1. Support for the allocation of interest scales to the four work task poles is provided by recent correlational studies involving various combinations of interest inventories [1; 7] and by analyses of interest inventory structure [3; 5; 7]. In addition, the interest scale allocations to work tasks indicated by the empirical data generally make good sense.

Counselors using any of the five interest inventories listed in Table 1 can supplement the regular reporting procedures with clinical assessment of interest patterns. For example, a student scoring highest on the computational and clerical scales of the Kuder General Interest Survey is probably expressing a preference for data work tasks, which suggests exploration of job families "up North" on the World-of-Work Map. If the persuasive scale is also high, the student might explore the business sales and management job cluster, and, more specifically, job families in and around region 2 of the map. For the 900,000 students taking the ACT each year, translation of work task preferences to a region on the map is automatic. The region is printed on the ACT Student Profile Report sent to high school counselors. The ACT student's booklet, *Planning for College*, provides several suggestions for using the map in occupational exploration.

Although there is more to the world of work than can be drawn on a piece of paper, the World-of-Work Map can provide a general sense of direction to persons engaged in career exploration. The map shows the location of the major "continents" in the work world, what the climate of each is like, and where each is located in relation to the others. It helps persons see how the specific occupations they are considering are related to work in general. Most important, it suggests regions of the world of work they may want to visit and explore.

References

1. American College Testing Program. *Handbook for the Career Planning Program, grades 8-11*. Iowa City, Iowa: Author, 1974.
2. Campbell, D. P. *Handbook for the Strong Vocational Interest Blank*. Stanford, Calif.: Stanford University Press, 1971.
3. Cole, N. S., & Hanson, G. R. An analysis of the structure of vocational interests. *Journal of Counseling Psychology*, 1971, *18*, 478-486.
4. Cottle, W. C. A factorial study of the Multiphasic, Strong, Kuder, and Bell inventories using a population of adult males. *Psychometrika*, 1950, *15*, 25-47.

5. Edwards, K. J., & Whitney, D. R. Structural analysis of Holland's personality types using factor and configural analysis. *Journal of Counseling Psychology,* 1972, *19,* 136-145.
6. Flanagan, J. C.; Shaycoft, M. F.; Richards, J. M., Jr.; & Claudy, J. C. *Five years after high school.* Palo Alto, Calif.: Project TALENT, 1971.
7. Hanson, G. R. *Assessing the interests of college youth: Summary of research and applications.* (ACT Research Report No. 67). Iowa City, Iowa: American College Testing Program, 1974.
8. Holland, J. L. *Making vocational choices.* Englewood Cliffs, N. J.: Prentice-Hall, 1973.
9. Holland, J. L.; Whitney, D. R.; Cole, N. S.; & Richards, J. M., Jr. *An empirical occupational classification derived from a theory of personality and intended for practice and research.* (ACT Research Report No. 29). Iowa City, Iowa: American College Testing Program, 1969.
10. Roe, A. *The psychology of occupations.* New York: Wiley, 1956.
11. Roe, A., & Klos, D. Occupational classification. *Counseling Psychologist,* 1969, *1,* 84-89.
12. U.S. Department of Labor, *Dictionary of occupational titles.* (3rd Ed.) Washington, D.C.: U.S. Government Printing Office, 1965.
13. U.S. Department of Labor. *Occupational Outlook Handbook; 1972-73 edition.* Washington, D.C: U.S. Government Printing Office, 1972-73.
14. U.S. Office of Education, Division of Vocational and Technical Education. *USOE career clusters.* Washington, D.C.: U.S. Government Printing Office, 1971. (Mimeograph)

TABLE 1

General Correspondence Between Work Task Preferences, ACT-OCS Job Clusters, and Interest Scales

	Interest inventory scales[a] most relevant to work task preferences		
Work task preferences (and associated job clusters)	SCII Theme Scales, VPI, SDS	Kuder GIS	OVIS
Data (Business Operations)	Conventional	Computational; Clerical	Numerical; Clerical Work
Data-People[b] (Business Sales & Management)	Enterprising	Persuasive	Customer Services; Sales Representative, Management and Supervision; Promotion and Communication
People (Social, Health, and Personal Services)	Social	Social Service	Caring for People; Nursing and Related, Teaching, Counseling, and Social Work
Ideas (Creative and Applied Arts; Natural, Social, and Medical Sciences)	Artistic; Investigative	Artistic; Literary; Scientific	Entertainment and Performance Arts; Music; Artistic; Literary; Medical; Applied Technology
Things (Technologies and Trades)	Realistic	Mechanical	Machine Work; Agriculture; Crafts and Precise Operations

[a] Scale abbreviations: Strong-Campbell Interest Inventory (SCII), Vocational Preference Inventory (VPI), Self-Directed Search (SDS); Kuder General Interest Survey (GIS); Ohio Vocational Interest Survey (OVIS).

[b] As shown by Figure 8, some job clusters involve combinations of work tasks. The Data-People combination is an example. It is emphasized here because several interest scales are relevant to this work task combination.

Descriptions of 12 Occupations

ARCHITECTURAL DRAFTER   RIA
WORK SETTING: INDOORS IN OFFICES OF ARCHITECTURAL FIRMS AND OF THE FEDERAL GOVERNMENT.
WORK TASKS: ARCHITECTURAL DRAFTERS PREPARE DETAILED DRAWINGS BASED ON ROUGH SKETCHES, SPECIFICATIONS, AND CALCULATIONS MADE BY ARCHITECTS. ARCHITECTURAL DRAFTERS:
-- ESTIMATE THE STRENGTH, QUALITY, QUANTITY, AND COST OF MATERIALS
-- TRANSLATE ARCHITECTS PRELIMINARY PLANS INTO DESIGN LAYOUTS (SENIOR DRAFTER)
-- DRAW EACH PART SHOWN ON THE LAYOUT, AND GIVE DIMENSIONS, MATERIALS AND OTHER INFORMATION TO MAKE THE DRAWING CLEAR AND COMPLETE (DETAILERS)
-- EXAMINE DRAWINGS FOR ERRORS IN COMPUTING OR RECORDING DIMENSIONS AND SPECIFICATIONS (CHECKERS)
-- MAKE MINOR CORRECTIONS AND TRACE DRAWINGS FOR REPRODUCTION (TRACERS).

COMPUTER PROGRAMMER   IRC
WORK SETTING: INDOORS IN OFFICES & COMPUTER ROOMS FOR MANUFACTURING FIRMS, BANKS AND INSURANCE COMPANIES, DATA PROCESSING SERVICE ORGANIZATIONS, GOVERNMENT AGENCIES, RESEARCH ORGANIZATIONS, AND MEDICAL AND EDUCATIONAL INSTITUTIONS.
WORK TASKS: COMPUTER PROGRAMMERS PREPARE THE INSTRUCTIONS THAT "TELL" THE COMPUTER HOW TO HANDLE INFORMATION AND SOLVE PROBLEMS. COMPUTER PROGRAMMERS:
-- DEVISE DETAILED PLANS FOR SOLVING SPECIFIC PROBLEMS OR TYPES OF PROBLEMS USING THE COMPUTER (APPLICATIONS PROGRAMMERS)
-- MAY WRITE INSTRUCTIONS THAT MAKE IT EASIER TO PROGRAM COMPUTERS AND PUT THEM TO WORK (SYSTEMS PROGRAMMER)
-- CHECK THEIR PROGRAMS TO MAKE SURE THEY ARE FREE FROM ERRORS.

BIOCHEMIST   IRS
WORK SETTING: INDOORS IN OFFICES AND LABORATORIES OF EDUCATIONAL AND MEDICAL INSTITUTIONS, PRIVATE INDUSTRY, RESEARCH ORGANIZATIONS, AND GOVERNMENT AGENCIES.
WORK TASKS: BIOCHEMISTS STUDY THE CHEMICAL COMPOSITION AND BEHAVIOR OF LIVING THINGS. BIOCHEMISTS:
-- MAY STUDY THE EFFECTS OF FOOD, HORMONES OR DRUGS ON VARIOUS ORGANISMS

-- WEIGH, FILTER, DISTILL, DRY AND GROW MICROORGANISMS
-- MAY DESIGN OR CONSTRUCT LABORATORY APPARATUS OR EQUIPMENT TO MEET THEIR INDIVIDUAL NEEDS
-- REPORT THE RESULTS OF THEIR RESEARCH IN PROFESSIONAL JOURNALS OR BEFORE SCIENTIFIC GROUPS
-- MAY TEACH IN COLLEGES OR UNIVERSITIES.

ADVERTISING COPYWRITER   ASI
WORK SETTING: INDOORS IN THE OFFICES OF ADVERTISERS, ADVERTISING AGENCIES, MEDIA, PUBLIC RELATIONS FIRMS, AND PROFESSIONAL AND TRADE ORGANIZATIONS.
WORK TASKS: ADVERTISING COPYWRITERS PROMOTE THE SALE OF GOODS AND SERVICES AS WELL AS THE ACCEPTANCE OF IDEAS. ADVERTISING COPYWRITERS:
-- RESEARCH NEEDED INFORMATION TO BECOME THOROUGHLY FAMILIAR WITH A PRODUCT OR SERVICE AND ITS POTENTIAL CUSTOMERS.
-- WRITE ADVERTISEMENTS AND TELEVISION AND RADIO COMMERCIALS.
-- MAY WRITE TRADE JOURNAL ARTICLES, PROMOTIONAL OR INFORMATIONAL BOOKLETS, SALES PROMOTION MATERIAL OR MERCHANDISING CAMPAIGNS.
-- MAY DISCUSS AN AD OR CAMPAIGN WITH THE ADVERTISER.
-- MAY HAVE TO EDIT OR REWRITE EXISTING COPY.

ACTOR/ACTRESS   AIS
WORK SETTING: INDOORS AND OUTDOORS ON STAGES, IN FILM AND TELEVISION STUDIOS, AND ANY OTHER LOCATIONS WHERE REQUIRED.
WORK TASKS: ACTORS/ACTRESSES USE SPEECH, MAKE-UP, COSTUMES AND GESTURES TO PORTRAY CHARACTERS IN PRODUCTIONS FOR THE STAGE, IN FILMS, AND ON TELEVISION OR RADIO. ACTORS/ACTRESSES:
-- ATTEND AUDITIONS FOR NEW PRODUCTIONS
-- ATTEND SPECIAL CLASSES (SUCH AS SINGING AND DANCING)
-- MEMORIZE LINES AND CUES
-- ATTEND REHEARSALS
-- TRAVEL IF A PLAY GOES ON TOUR OR IF A FILM OR COMMERCIAL IS DONE "ON LOCATION"
-- MAY HAVE TO WORK IN OTHER JOBS SINCE EMPLOYMENT IS USUALLY IRREGULAR.

COUNSELOR   SAE
WORK SETTING: INDOORS IN OFFICES IN A BROAD RANGE OF SETTINGS.
WORK TASKS: HELP PEOPLE TO UNDERSTAND THEMSELVES AND THEIR ENVIRONMENT SO THEY CAN SET AND ACHIEVE REASONABLE AND SATISFYING GOALS;
-- MAY AID STUDENTS IN PERSONAL AND SOCIAL DEVELOPMENT AND HELP THEM TO PLAN FOR AND ACHIEVE EDUCATIONAL AND VOCATIONAL GOALS (SCHOOL COUNSELOR);
-- MAY HELP PHYSICALLY, MENTALLY OR SOCIALLY HANDICAPPED PEOPLE TO BECOME MORE SELF-RELIANT MEMBERS OF THEIR COMMUNITIES (REHABILITATION COUNSELOR);
-- MAY HELP ALL KINDS OF PEOPLE IN ALL AGE GROUPS TO PLAN THEIR CAREERS AND FIND SUITABLE EMPLOYMENT (EMPLOYMENT COUNSELOR);
-- MAY HELP STUDENTS TO EXAMINE THEIR INTERESTS, ABILITIES AND GOALS AND EXPLORE CAREER ALTERNATIVES AND FOLLOW THROUGH WITH THEIR CAREER CHOICES (EMPLOYMENT REPRESENTATIVE OR COLLEGE PLACEMENT COUNSELOR).

NURSE, LICENSED PRACTICAL   SAI
WORK SETTING: IN LARGE AND SMALL INSTITUTIONS THAT CARE FOR THE MENTALLY OR PHYSICALLY ILL OR HANDICAPPED;
-- IN FACTORIES, SCHOOLS, CAMPS, DOCTOR'S OFFICES AND IN PRIVATE HOMES.
WORK TASKS: ASSIST PROFESSIONALLY TRAINED MEDICAL PERSONNEL IN THE CARE AND TREATMENT OF THE PHYSICALLY OR MENTALLY ILL AND THE HANDICAPPED;
-- CHECK TEMPERATURE, PULSE AND BLOOD PRESSURE;
-- MAKE PATIENT COMFORTABLE AND ASSIST IN PERSONAL HYGIENE AND CLEANLINESS;
-- PREPARE PATIENTS FOR EXAMINATIONS AND OPERATIONS;
-- MAY DISPENSE MEDICATION, GIVE BLOOD TRANSFUSIONS OR INTRAVENOUS FEEDING;
-- MAY DO SIMPLE LAB TESTS;
-- PERFORM OTHER DUTIES REQUIRING TECHNICAL KNOWLEDGE BUT NOT PROFESSIONAL TRAINING, TO FREE OTHERS FOR MORE SPECIALIZED TASKS.

NURSE, REGISTERED   SIA
WORK SETTING: MOST NURSES WORK IN HOSPITALS, BUT OTHERS WORK IN HOMES, CLINICS, LARGE BUSINESS ESTABLISHMENTS, CLASSROOMS, MENTAL HOSPITALS, SCHOOLS, NURSING HOMES, REHABILITATION CENTERS, DOCTOR'S OR DENTIST'S OFFICES OR ON MILITARY BASES AT HOME OR ABROAD.
WORK TASKS: DUTIES VARY WITH THE CHOSEN SPECIALTY, BUT A STATE LICENSE QUALIFIES A NURSE TO:

-- OBSERVE SYMPTOMS AND REPORT THEM TO THE ATTENDING PHYSICIAN;
-- DISPENSE PRESCRIBED MEDICATION, GIVE INJECTIONS AND CHANGE DRESSINGS;
-- TAKE AND RECORD TEMPERATURE, PULSE, AND RESPIRATION RATE;
-- PREPARE AND STERILIZE INSTRUMENTS;
-- MAKE SURE PATIENTS ARE AS COMFORTABLE AS POSSIBLE;
-- PERFORM OTHER PATIENT-CARE DUTIES AS AUTHORIZED BY THE ATTENDING PHYSICIAN.

SALES MANAGER   ESC
WORK SETTING: USUALLY INDOORS AT SALES OFFICE, STORE, SHOWROOMS OR IN CORPORATE OFFICES.
WORK TASKS: DIRECT SALES DEPARTMENT STAFFING, TRAINING AND PERFORMANCE EVALUATION;
-- COORDINATE SALES DISTRIBUTION THROUGH ESTABLISHMENT OF SALES TERRITORIES, QUOTAS, AND GOALS;
-- REVIEW MARKET ANALYSES TO DETERMINE CUSTOMER NEEDS, VOLUME POTENTIAL, PRICE SCHEDULES,
-- EVALUATE DEALER SALES AND ASSIST DEALERS THROUGH TRAINING PROGRAMS AND SALES PROMOTION.

REAL ESTATE AGENT   ECS
WORK SETTING: IN A REAL ESTATE OFFICE, AT THE SITE OF PROPERTIES FOR SALE OR RENT, AND IN AN AUTOMOBILE TRAVELING FROM ONE SETTING TO ANOTHER.
WORK TASKS: SELL, BUY, RENT AND MANAGE LAND, HOUSES AND COMMERCIAL BUILDINGS;
-- SOLICIT BOOKINGS OF RESIDENTIAL, COMMERCIAL OR AGRICULTURAL PROPERTIES FOR SALE OR RENT, AND VISIT THE PROPERTY TO BECOME FAMILIAR WITH IT;
-- ADVISE THE OWNER ABOUT THE ASKING PRICE, AND NEGOTIATE A CONTRACT ALLOWING THEMSELVES A PERCENTAGE OF THE TOTAL SELLING PRICE WHEN IT IS SOLD;
-- ANALYZE EACH PROPERTY AND FIT IT TO THE NEEDS OF PROSPECTIVE CUSTOMERS;
-- ARRANGE FOR POTENTIAL BUYERS TO VISIT THE PROPERTY AND EMPHASIZE POINTS OF INTEREST, INCLUDING TAX RATES, ZONING REGULATIONS AND INSURANCE NEEDS;
-- NEGOTIATE PRICE, PREPARE FORMAL SALES CONTRACT, ARRANGE MORTGAGE LOANS AND ADVISE OWNERS ABOUT SUCH THINGS AS TITLE SEARCH AND TITLE INSURANCE.

ACCOUNTANT   CES
WORK SETTING: INDOORS IN THE OFFICES OF THEIR EMPLOYERS OR THE OFFICES OF THEIR CLIENTS.
WORK TASKS: ACCOUNTANTS PREPARE AND ANALYZE FINANCIAL REPORTS.
THE 4 PRIMARY TYPES OF ACCOUNTANTS INCLUDE:
PUBLIC ACCOUNTANT: HELP PEOPLE TO MANAGE THEIR MONEY. THEY SET UP AND KEEP ACCOUNTING SYSTEMS FOR BUSINESSES, AS WELL AS PREPARE BUDGETS, STUDY COMPANY OPERATIONS, DO AUDITS, GIVE OPINIONS ON REPORTS, AND PREPARE GOVERNMENT FORMS.
MANAGEMENT ACCOUNTANT: HELP MANAGEMENT PLAN AND CONTROL COMPANY ACTIVITIES. THEY TAKE PART IN EVERY STAGE OF PROBLEM SOLVING AND DECISION MAKING IN BUSINESS.
GOVERNMENT ACCOUNTANT: REVIEW AGENCY RECORDS AND THE RECORDS OF PERSONS AND PRIVATE FIRMS WHO MUST FOLLOW GOVERNMENT RULES AND REGULATIONS.
ACCOUNTING TEACHER: STUDY, ORGANIZE AND TEACH ACCOUNTING PRINCIPLES AND METHODS TO STUDENTS AT THE SECONDARY AND COLLEGE LEVELS.

BANK TELLER   CSE
WORK SETTING: INDOORS IN BANKS AND OTHER FINANCIAL INSTITUTIONS.
WORK TASKS: BANK TELLERS ARE REPRESENTATIVES OF THE BANK WHO DEAL WITH THE PUBLIC. BANK TELLERS:
-- CASH CUSTOMERS CHECKS
-- HANDLE DEPOSITS AND WITHDRAWALS FROM CHECKING AND SAVINGS ACCOUNTS
-- COUNT CASH ON HAND BEFORE AND AFTER BANKING HOURS
-- FILL OUT SETTLEMENT SHEETS AND BALANCE THE DAY'S ACCOUNTS AFTER BANKING HOURS.

Session 5
Summary

Objective	Suggested Activities	Suggested Time	Materials
1. To define *interest* and *skill*	Mini-lecture	10 min.	None
2. To identify present interests and skills related to life roles	Complete Career Interests and Skills Assessment Worksheet	30 min.	Career Interests and Skills Assessment Worksheet, one copy for each participant (not included in *Career Planning Guide*). See Appendix A of this manual.
3. To develop awareness of the possibility of transfer of skills and interests from role to role and from occupation to occupation	Class discussion and further work with Career Assessment Worksheet	20 min.	Same as above
4. To observe career development and choice in the lives of others	Selected group members give reports on their reading.	40 min.	None

Homework

Complete Exercise 5, Exploring Occupations by Assessing Your Experiences and Skills.

Objectives and Activities

Objective 1: To define *interest* and *skill*

Mini-lecture

1. An *interest* is a strong preference to do one thing rather than another. A *skill* is the ability to do something well.

2. Interests are formed through the reinforcement of activities which we engage in. In other words, life situations offer a variety of different kinds of activities to different people. If the individual finds that he/she can perform these activities well and is reinforced by intrinsic and extrinsic rewards for doing these activities, they become *interests*.

   Usually people seek to gain competence or skill in those things in which they are interested. Pursuing interests with motivation and frequency develops skills.

3. Of the various pieces of self-information which are assessed in this program (i.e., interests, skills, abilities, values, self-concept), the one which is most likely to predict what individuals will be doing ten years from now is *interests*. For that reason, the analysis of interests should be considered the most important factor in vocational choice.

4. Interests, as well as skills, change, especially in the adolescent years. Interests tend to stabilize in the mid-twenties, although change throughout life is now a normal phenomenon.

Suggested time: 10 minutes

Materials: None

Objective 2: To identify present interests and skills related to life roles and skills for future development

Suggested activities:

A. The leader asks participants to complete Career Interests and Skills Assessment Worksheet, which is passed out at this time.

When all participants have finished, ask them to go back and circle all interests and skills (both possessed now and to be developed) which they wish to use in a future Worker role.

B. The leader asks individuals to volunteer to report what they have entered on the worksheet. Questions like the following are used to stimulate discussion:

1. Do you see a consistent pattern of interests across your life roles? of skills?
2. Do you see some interests in nonwork roles that you would like to transfer to the Worker role? some skills?
3. Do these patterns indicate that you may be ready for a vocational choice? Why or why not?
4. What skills do you want to develop in any of the roles?
5. How can you develop these skills?

C. The leader indicates that the next assignment will provide a more structured and detailed way of assessing interests and skills. Today's exercise is being used as an introduction and will be reviewed again later in light of more detailed assessment.

Suggested time: 30 minutes

Materials: Career Interests and Skills Assessment Worksheet (copies made from Appendix A of this manual)

Objective 3: To develop awareness of the possibility of transfer of skills and interests from role to role and from occupation to occupation

Suggested activities:

A. Participants are asked to draw arrows from any interests or skills (now possessed or to be developed) which they would like to transfer to different roles. For example, a person might now have a skill and/or interest in tennis associated with the "Leisurite" role. This interest and skill might be transferred to the Worker role by finding a full-time position as a tennis pro or owner of a tennis club. A skill of bookkeeping or accurate accounting developed in the Homemaker role might be transferred to the Worker role. Interest in working face to face with people might be transferred from the Worker role to the Citizen role. As soon as participants are finished with their worksheets, they are asked to exchange the worksheet with another member of the group.

B. Participants are asked to list as many occupations as they can think of on the other's worksheet which will make use of all or most of the interests and skills circled. When this process is finished, the worksheets should be returned to their owners. Discussion follows about the transferability of interests and skills to other roles of the career and from occupation to occupation within the Worker role. The leader might use questions like the following:

1. What examples have you experienced or seen on worksheets which indicate that interests and skills are transferable from role to role and from occupation to occupation?

2. How might this fact help an adult who is interested in making a career change?

3. What kinds of circumstances in life might prompt people to want to transfer interests and skills across roles or from occupation to occupation?

Suggested time: 20 minutes

Materials: Career Interests and Skills Assessment Worksheet

Objective 4: To observe career development and choice in the lives of others

Suggested activities:

A. Participants are asked to provide an 8-10 minute oral report on the life of the person whom they have read about for today's assignment. These reports should emphasize the following:

1. The influences on this person's vocational choice

2. The roles being played and the harmony or conflict among them

3. The self-concept of the person and how this was developed, strengthened, and/or diminished

4. The interests, skills (talents, abilities), and experiences of the person and how these were developed, reinforced, or discouraged

5. The effects of all of the above on vocational choice and happiness

6. Lessons to be learned from this person's life

B. Participants should be encouraged to question the presenter, and the leader should be active in assisting the group to make good inferences about vocational choice and career development.

Suggested time: 40 minutes

Materials: Reports assigned for homework

Homework assignment: Complete Exercise 5, Exploring Occupations by Assessing Your Experiences and Skills, in Chapter 6 of the *Career Planning Guide.*

Session 6

Objective

The single objective of this session is to administer the abilities measures of the Career Planning Program, Form H (copyright 1976 by The American College Testing Program). The purpose in administering the instrument is to assist individuals to relate abilities to clusters of occupations in order to identify feasible ones for further exploration.

Materials Needed for Administration

CPP Booklet, Form H (one for each person)
Self-Scoring Answer Folder for CPP Ability Tests, Form H (one for each person)
Sharpened No. 2 black-lead pencils (one for each person)
A stopwatch or test timing clock

Time Considerations

The total testing time for the CPP is 74 minutes. In addition, approximately 23 minutes are required for distribution of materials and directions. Therefore, the administration of the test *will require the total session time.* The chart below gives the exact testing time for each timed section and the estimated time for distribution and collection of materials and for instructions.

Tasks	Exact Time	Estimated Time
1. Pass out test booklets, pencils, and Self-Scoring Answer Folders		10 minutes
2. Administer Language Usage test	**8 minutes** for test-taking	3 additional minutes for directions
3. Administer Reading Skills test	**20 minutes** for test-taking	2 additional minutes for directions
4. Administer Clerical Skills test	**6 minutes** for test-taking	3 additional minutes for directions
5. **Break**		10 minutes
6. Administer Numerical Skills test	**18 minutes** for test-taking	1 additional minute for directions
7. Administer Mechanical Reasoning test	**14 minutes** for test-taking	1 additional minute for directions
8. Administer Space Relations test	**8 minutes** for test-taking	3 additional minutes for directions
	74 minutes	33 minutes
	Total time required = 107 minutes	

Instructions for Administering the Career Planning Program

A complete set of instructions for administering the CPP follows. All instructions enclosed in boxes are to be read aloud by the test administrator, **except** italicized instructions in parentheses, which are for the administrator's information only.

After all participants are seated and you have their attention, pass out the Self-Scoring Answer Folders (Form H) and say:

> Today you will be given the ACT Career Planning Program (or CPP). You must use only a soft, black-lead pencil. Is there anyone who does *not* have a soft, black-lead pencil? *(Pause to distribute pencils if necessary.)*
>
> Do not make any marks on your answer folders until I tell you to do so.

After you have determined that all participants have both a pencil and an answer folder, say:

> These answer folders will be scored by you. Special care must be used in marking them so that you will compute your scores correctly.
>
> I will now distribute the CPP booklets. Do not break the seal or open your booklet until I tell you to do so. When you receive your booklet, turn to the back cover and study the directions printed there.

Distribute the test booklets by handing one to each person. Keep an exact record of the number of booklets distributed. When everyone has one, read the following directions which appear on the back cover of the booklet:

> Now I will read the directions from the back cover of your booklet.
>
> The Career Planning Program is designed to help you make plans for your education and future career. The booklet is divided into 9 short units in which information is collected about you, your background, your interests, and your skills. You will use the answer folder provided to answer all the questions in the CPP booklet. The answer folder includes sections which match 6 of the units in this booklet. We will make use of only 6 of the 10 sections in the test booklet. For each question in these 6 sections there is a matching row of rectangles on the answer folder numbered the same as the

> question. Make a heavy black mark in the rectangle that corresponds to the answer you have selected.
>
> Use a soft-lead pencil and make marks like those on page 2 of the answer booklet. The important thing is to make a heavy mark that can be read easily.
>
> If you change your mind about an answer, be sure to put an X through the rectangle as illustrated on page 2 of the answer booklet. Make certain each time that your mark is placed in the row with the same number as the question.

When all individuals have had time to print their names, say:

> Break the seal on your booklet and open it to page 2.
>
> The main purpose of the ACT Career Planning Program is to help you identify and explore your career options so that you can plan wisely for your future education and work. The CPP measures several abilities that are important in education and work. Your CPP report will help you tie this information together with your interests, experiences, and skills in making your career plans.
>
> Skip Units 1 and 2 and turn to Unit 3 on page 9.
>
> Unit 3, "Language Usage," on page 9 is the first of six short units that will measure some of your present abilities. These units will enable you to focus your attention on jobs requiring abilities and skills like your own.
>
> As you complete these short tests, try to answer every item. If you are uncertain about an answer, mark the one you feel is most nearly correct. Read all directions and listen to instructions carefully.
>
> Once work on a unit is begun, no questions may be answered.
>
> Now read the directions for Unit 3 silently as I read them aloud.
>
> This unit consists of 10 sentences, each having 4 underlined parts. Some underlined parts are correct as they are; others are incorrect. Incorrect parts involve common errors in the use of the English language. For each underlined part mark "C" if it is correct and "I" if incorrect. You should assume that any part of a sentence which is not underlined is grammatically correct. Mark your answers in the first section of your answer folder. Now, study the samples below.

When the participants have had between 1 and 2 minutes to study
the samples, set the time for **exactly 8 minutes** and say:

> You will have 8 minutes to work on this unit. Work quickly and carefully. Turn the page and begin work.

When **exactly 8 minutes** have elapsed, say:

> STOP WORK.

Then say:

> Turn to Unit 4, the "Reading Skills" unit, on page 11. *(Pause.)* Read the directions silently as I read them aloud.
>
> This unit has 5 passages, each followed by 8 questions. Read the passage, then choose the best answer to each question. You may look back at the passage as often as you wish. Mark your answers in the second section of your answer folder. *(Pause.)*

Set the time for **20 minutes;** then say:

> You will have 20 minutes to work on this unit. Work quickly and carefully. Turn the page and begin work.

When **exactly 20 minutes** have elapsed, say:

> STOP WORK. Put your pencils down.
>
> Skip Unit 5 on page 18, the "Vocational Interest Profile" unit. *(Pause.)*
>
> Turn to Unit 6 on page 19, the "Clerical Skills" unit. *(Pause.)* Read the directions silently as I read them aloud.
>
> The National Fruit Company sends packages of fruit to destinations all over the United States. You will be given a list of 35 shipments made during a typical business day. The SHIPPING LIST gives the destination of the shipment, the distance it is to be sent, and its weight. After you read the distance and weight from the SHIPPING LIST, you will look up the TRANSPORTATION COST in TABLE I. In TABLE II, you will find the interval that

> includes this figure in the column labeled COST. Next to that interval you will find the letter which is the correct ANSWER. Mark your answers in the Unit 6 section of your answer folder. Now, work through the sample below. *(Pause.)*
>
> In the sample, a shipment is going to Cleveland, a distance of 1106 miles. The package weighs 16 pounds.
>
> In TABLE I, under Distance in Miles, you see that 1106 falls in the interval 1000-1499, which is in the third row and is underlined. Now, move across that row until you reach the column labeled 15-19, the interval that includes 16, the weight of the shipment to Cleveland. The figure you find there is the TRANSPORTATION COST, in this case $1.50. Next look at TABLE II. Since $1.50 falls between $1.41 and $1.65, the ANSWER to the sample is D.

Set the time for **6 minutes;** then say:

> You will have 6 minutes to work on this unit. Work quickly and carefully. Turn the page and begin work.

After **6 minutes** have elapsed, say:

> STOP WORK. Put your answer sheets inside your test booklet, and close the booklet. We will now take a 10-minute break. Please return by (time).

After the break, say:

> Turn to Unit 7 on page 21, the "Numerical Skills" unit. *(Pause.)* Read the directions silently as I read them aloud.
>
> This unit has 36 questions, each of which is followed by 5 possible answers. You are to choose the correct answer to each question. For some questions, the fifth choice for an answer will be "Not given." Whenever you think none of the first 4 possible answers is correct, mark "Not given" as your answer. Mark your answers in the fourth section of your answer folder. DO YOUR FIGURING IN THE SPACE PROVIDED NEXT TO EACH ITEM.

Set the time for **18 minutes**; then say:

> You will have 18 minutes to work on this unit. Work quickly and carefully. Turn the page and begin work.

When exactly **18 minutes** have elapsed, say:

> STOP WORK.

Then say:

> Turn to Unit 8, the "Mechanical Reasoning" unit at the bottom of page 25. Read the directions silently as I read them aloud.
>
> This unit has 34 questions, each followed by 3 possible answers. Read each question and study the drawing beside it; then select the correct answer. Mark your answers in the fifth section of your answer folder.

Set the time for **14 minutes**; then say:

> You will have 14 minutes to work on this unit. Work quickly and carefully. Turn the page and begin work.

After **14 minutes** have elapsed, say:

> STOP WORK.

Then say:

> Turn to Unit 9 on page 33, the "Space Relations" unit. Read the directions silently as I read them aloud.
>
> Each of the stacks of blocks in the Space Relations unit is made up of **identical** blocks. Five of the blocks are lettered. You are to determine the number of blocks that each lettered block touches. Blocks having **surfaces** (tops, bottoms, sides, or ends) in contact are counted as touching. Do **NOT** count blocks as touching if they have only edges or corners in contact.

> Count the number of blocks touching the lettered blocks. Then use the answer key below to select your answers.
>
> If a block is touching 3 or fewer blocks, the answer is 3.
> If a block is touching 4 blocks, the answer is 4.
> If a block is touching 5 blocks, the answer is 5.
> If a block is touching 6 or more blocks, the answer is 6.
>
> Mark your answers in the last section of your answer folder. Now study the samples below.

When the participants have had at least 1 but no more than 2 minutes to do the sample, set the time for exactly **8 minutes** and say:

> You will have 8 minutes to work on this unit. Work quickly and carefully. Turn the page and begin work.

When **exactly 8 minutes** have elapsed, say:

> STOP WORK.

Then say:

> Close your test booklet. Close your answer folder. Your test booklet will now be collected. Keep the answer folders so that you can score them for next week.

Collect the test booklets. Count the booklets carefully to see that all are returned.

Session 7
Summary

Objective	Suggested Activities	Suggested Time	Material
1. To process the exercises related to interests, experiences, and skills	Discussion	15 min.	Exercises 4A and 5 of *Career Planning Guide*
2. To process the Career Planning Program (CPP) Ability Tests	Discussion	20 min.	Self-Scoring Answer Folder for the CPP
3. To assist individuals to integrate the identification of occupations by interests, experiences, skills, and abilities	Add information to World-of-Work Summary Sheet	20 min.	World-of-Work Summary Sheet in *Career Planning Guide*
4. To introduce the topic of stereotyping	The New Frontier exercise	40 min.	Copies of the New Frontier exercise, Appendix A of this manual

Homework

Read Chapter 7 of the *Career Planning Guide* and complete Exercise 6, Stereotyping in Employment, with either of the two options described.

Supplementary Readings

Berliner, D. *Want a Job? Get some experience. Want experience? Get a Job.* New York: Amacon, 1978.

Career Planning Program Counselor's Manual. Iowa City, Iowa: The American College Testing Program, 1981.

User's Resource Book: Vocational Interest, Experience, and Skill Assessment. Iowa City, Iowa: The American College Testing Program, 1978.

Resource Materials

Films: "A Different Drum", Brigham Young University, Media Marketing, W170 Stadium, Provo, UT 84602.

Learning Kit: Sex Fairness in Career Guidance. Abt Publications, 55 Wheeler Street, Cambridge, MA 02138.

Objectives and Activities

Objective 1: To process the exercises related to interests, experiences, and skills

Suggested activities:

A. The leader facilitates the discussion of the exercises with questions like the following:

1. Which region(s) of the World-of-Work Map were suggested by your interest inventory? your self-rating of skills? your experience?

2. What are some of the interests and skills suggested by these results?

3. Were the regions different by interests, experiences, and skills? If so, how do you account for this?

4. Were the results different for skills you possess and skills you want to use in an occupation? If so, why?

5. Did you find occupations through doing this assignment that you are interested in exploring further?

6. Were the results of doing these exercises consistent with the interests and skills you circled on the Career Interests and Skills Assessment Worksheet?

Suggested time: 15 minutes

Materials: Exercises 4A (or 4B in Appendix C) and 5 of the *Career Planning Guide*

B. Participants are asked to turn to the World-of-Work Summary Sheet (Appendix A) of the *Career Planning Guide* and to record an **I** (for *interests*) in the region in which the interest inventory score fell (Exercise 4A); and an **E** (for *experiences*) and an **S** (for *skills*) in the appropriate regions selected in Exercise 5 of the *Guide*.

Objective 2: To process the Career Planning Program (CPP) Ability Tests

Suggested activity:

The leader explains that the Career Interests and Skills Assessment Worksheet was an unsophisticated way of identifying interest and skills. The Interests, Skills, and Experiences exercise was a more sophisticated way of assisting individuals to view their skills and experiences in a systematic way. The items in this exercise simply assist individuals to rate themselves from their personal, subjective point of view. The CPP, on the other hand, attempts to measure abilities in a more objective way and to compare the ability of one individual to that of others in a comparable "norm group." Individuals are asked to turn to the World-of-Work Summary Sheet again and to record an **A** (for *abilities*) in the regions of higher abililty scores. The material on pages 67-71 of this manual provides additional information for the leader. Group participation is encouraged by asking the following questions:

1. Which regions of the World-of-Work Map were suggested by your highest ability scores?

2. Were some abilities significantly higher (2 stanines or more) for you than others?

3. Was there an overlap of regions identified by self-assessment of interests, skills, experiences, and by your ability scores on the CPP?

4. Did the Abilities Tests help you to identify any new occupations for exploration?

5. Do you have any questions about the scoring or interpretation of the CPP?

Suggested time: 20 minutes

Materials: Self-Scoring Answer Folder for the CPP

Objective 3: To help individuals integrate the identification of potential occupations by interests, experiences, skills, and abilities

Suggested activity:

The group leader asks participants to turn to page 125, the World-of-Work Summary Sheet, in Appendix A of the *Career Planning Guide*. Participants should have already recorded the letters I (for interests), E (experiences), S (skills), and A (abilities) on the map. The group leader asks participants the following questions:

1. Did all four scores fall in the same region for anyone? (This would be unusual since this represents a very high level of consistency.)

2. Did all four scores fall in two or three adjacent regions for anyone?

3. Were the four scores scattered around the circle for anyone? If so, can you give any explanation for this?

4. Do these summary results seem consistent with what you know about yourself? If not, why not?

Suggested time: 20 minutes

Materials: World-of-Work Summary Sheet of the *Career Planning Guide*

Objective 4: To introduce the topic of stereotyping

Suggested activities:

A. Participants are asked to form groups of five to seven members and select a leader. The leader then passes out The New Frontier exercise (in Appendix A of this manual) and asks that each person read it and complete the individual selections. Then each leader works with his or her team to reach group consensus about the list of chosen candidates.

B. After about 20 minutes, the experience is processed as follows:

1. The leader of each group is asked to report which eight persons his or her group has decided to take to The New Frontier. The leader should summarize the report of all groups on the board.

2. The leader encourages discussion with the following questions and any others that might occur:

   a. Which individuals were taken to The New Frontier by all groups? Why? Which values and/or stereotypes are being expressed by these decisions?

   b. Which individuals were not taken by all groups? Why? Which values or stereotypes are being expressed by these decisions?

c. Did you notice that certain individuals were always called "he" or "she" in the group discussion? Why? Which occupational titles were assumed to be "male" and which were assumed to be "female?"

C. The leader comments that the program has been focusing, to this point, on factors of vocational choice (such as interests, skills, abilities) which are *internal* to an individual. It will now give attention to some factors that are (at least partly) *external* to the individual, beginning with stereotyping. The assignment for the next session will provide an opportunity for participants to talk with one individual who may have experienced the effect of stereotyping or to read about trends in stereotyping. The assignment is explained on page 61 of the *Career Planning Guide*.

Suggested time: 40 minutes

Materials: The New Frontier exercise in Appendix A of this manual

Homework assignment: Read Chapter 7 of the *Career Planning Guide* and complete Exercise 6, Stereotyping in Employment, with either of the two options described on page 61.

Background

(Note: For more detailed information on the interpretation of the interests, experiences, and skills inventories, see *Vocational Interest, Experience, and Skill Assessment: User's Reference Book*, Iowa City, Iowa: The American College Testing Program, 1978.)

This session of the Personal Life and Career Planning Program helps participants explore occupations by several means: an interest inventory, self-assessed experiences and skills, and measured abilities. In exploring occupations, *all* these different measured factors are significant and should be considered in any interpretation of occupational choices.

Interest Inventory

The American College Testing Program's 60-item interest inventory, called UNIACT, is provided to participants as Exercise 4A, pages 41-45, of the *Career Planning Guide*. Both Roe (1956) and Holland (1973) have provided research data which indicate that both occupations and vocational interests can be represented by a relatively small number of groups or dimensions. The ACT interest inventory uses the typology of John Holland (1973), briefly summarized on pages 28-29 of this manual. Research at ACT on the structure of interests indicates that when the effects of response set are eliminated, most of what is measured by scales assessing Holland's six types can be summarized by the DATA/IDEAS and THINGS/PEOPLE work task dimensions (see Figure 9). UNIACT provides two scales (30 items each) which assess the DATA/IDEAS and THINGS/PEOPLE dimensions directly. Thus the instrument reports an individual's interests (work-related activity preferences) on the same two dimensions used to describe basic work tasks associated with occupations. The score grid on page 43 of the *Guide* translates an individual's scores on these two dimensions into one of 13 regions on the World-of-Work Map. This region number summarizes the person's work-related activity preferences according to general orientation to data, ideas, people, or things.

A 90-item version of UNIACT is also included as Exercise 4B in Appendix C of the *Career Planning Guide,* with instructions for its administration in Appendix C of this manual. This instrument provides two methods of interpretation: (1) a norm-referenced Holland code and (2) a World-of-Work region. If, as leader, you prefer to have participants receive a Holland code which can be compared by percentile or stanine to codes received by a large national sample of college-age students, you will want to assign Exercise 4B instead of 4A. Table C.1 in Appendix C of the *Career Planning Guide* provides you with the information you need to enable participants to understand how their interests compare in strength with those of a nationally representative sample of young adults. You may want to duplicate the "Scoring Instructions" worksheet in Exercise 4B (Appendix C of this manual) for use in group interpretation of the Holland code. Table C.2 (Appendix C of the *Career Planning Guide*) provides you with the information required to convert the Holland code derived from the 90-item UNIACT into a World-of-Work region, so that participants can directly relate their interests to this schema.

DATA/IDEAS DIMENSION

Data (facts, records, files, numbers, systematic procedures for facilitating goods/services consumption by people). "Data activities" involve *impersonal processes* such as recording, verifying, transmitting, and organizing facts or data representing goods and services. Purchasing agents, accountants, and air traffic controllers work *mainly* with data.	**Ideas** (abstractions, theories, knowledge, insights, and new ways of expressing something—for example, with words, equations, or music). "Ideas activities" involve *intrapersonal processes* such as creating, discovering, interpreting, and synthesizing abstractions or implementing applications of abstractions. Scientists, musicians, and philosophers work *mainly* with ideas.

PEOPLE/THINGS DIMENSION

People (no alternative terms). "People activities" involve *interpersonal processes* such as helping, informing, serving, persuading, entertaining, motivating, and directing—in general, producing a change in human behavior. Teachers, salespersons, and nurses work *mainly* with people.	**Things** (machines, mechanisms, materials, tools, physical and biological processes). "Things activities" involve *nonpersonal processes* such as producing, transporting, servicing, and repairing. Bricklayers, farmers, and engineers work *mainly* with things.

All occupations involve some work with data, ideas, people, and things. The examples listed above were chosen with an emphasis on the primary purpose or focus of the job activities. For example, a scientist may work with data, but the primary purpose is *not* to produce or handle data, rather it is to create or apply scientific knowledge. Likewise, an accountant may work with ideas, but the ultimate goal is *not* to create ideas, rather it is to organize, record, and verify data in a systematic manner.

Figure 9. Definitions of the DATA/IDEAS and PEOPLE/THINGS Work/Task Dimensions.

To interpret the Holland code derived from the 90-item UNIACT, two concepts are particularly important—consistency and differentiation. *Consistency* refers to the combination of the first two letters of the code and the degree to which these letters are related on the Holland hexagon. Referring to the hexagon on page 28 of this manual, the reader will note that three levels of consistency are possible:

High consistency—The first two letters of the code are "next door" to each other on the hexagon, such as RI, IA, and SE. This means that primary interests are highly related to each other.

Medium consistency—The first two letters of the code are one point away from each other on the hexagon, such as RA, IS, and CI. This means that the individual's primary interests are somewhat different from each other.

Low consistency—The first two letters of the code are across the hexagon from each other, such as CA, SR, and EI. This means that the individual's two areas of primary interest are very different from each other. It may be difficult to find jobs which combine such diverse interests.

Differentiation refers to the point (or stanine) difference between the highest scale and the lowest. Ideally, there would be a marked difference. In practical terms, this means that the individual has an area or areas of interest which are substantially stronger than others. This may signal readiness for vocational choice.

Three patterns of differentiation are common, and each suggests a different interpretation. The three "profiles" may be described as follows:

High flat profile—Most or all of the six scales are in stanines 7, 8, and 9.

> *Interpretation:* Individual sees self as multi-interested and multi-talented. Since few jobs combine all of these interests, the individual will have to select which interests to implement in the Worker role and which to implement in other life roles. The job market and personal values will help make this decision.

Low flat profile—Most or all of the six scales are in stanines 1, 2, and 3.

> *Interpretation:* Individual does not have well-defined interests or self-rated abilities. May have had limited life experience, or at least in exposure to World-of-Work opportunities. Is probably not ready for vocational choice. Needs counselor assistance in learning about alternatives and how to gain experience related to the six Holland types.

Well-differentiated profile—At least one scale is in stanine 7, 8, or 9, and at least one is in stanine 1, 2, or 3.

> *Interpretation:* Individual does have one (or more) areas of significant interest and self-rated ability. May be ready to seriously explore occupations which are coded with letters of the highest scales.

The interest items used in UNIACT were carefully chosen to minimize sex-related difference in responses. Hence, the stereotypic divergencies in the career options, typically suggested to males and females by raw scores or by standard scores based on combined sex norms, are minimized. Item content emphasizes relatively familiar career-related activities (many of which counselees may have experienced firsthand) rather than abstract job titles subject to sex-role stereotypes. The rationale for UNIACT, and its development and psychometric characteristics (including reliability and validity information), are described by Lamb and Prediger (1981).

Though UNIACT scores should be viewed as one good way to assist individuals to *find direction for career exploration,* they should not be viewed as predictive. Program participants should be encouraged to explore carefully all occupations in the region where their interest inventory score falls, and all occupations in adjacent regions. If such exploration still does not identify occupations of interest to the participant, exploration should branch out to regions adjacent to these three.

Self-Assessment of Experiences

Exercise 5 of the *Career Planning Guide*—"Exploring Occupations by Assessing Your Experiences and Skills"—attempts to tap into specific experiences individuals may have had and to relate these to the four dimensions of the World-of-Work Map: working with DATA, with PEOPLE, with THINGS, and with IDEAS. Individuals are asked to evaluate their experiences and prioritize the four areas for exploration. The items developed by The American College Testing Program for each of the four work dimensions are inferred from the theoretical framework of the World-of-Work Map and the principal occupational tasks associated with each of the four dimensions. The items have been extensively tested by ACT.

Self-assessment of experiences is one way of assisting individuals to select occupations for exploration. This method might be particularly helpful for an individual who does not seem to have clearly defined interests or who wants to change occupations without major retraining. The method might not be useful for an individual who wants to make a radical change from what he or she has been doing.

Self-Assessment of Skills

Skill can be defined as *the ability to perform specific tasks well,* and implies an already tested and proven ability to perform. Each of the four dimensions of the World-of-Work Map requires a different set of skills for successful performance in the occupations assigned to that dimension. Exercise 5 of the *Career Planning Guide* lists these skills and asks individuals to select those which they believe they have and those which they wish to use in an occupation. As the next step in the exercise—"Analyzing Your Skills"—individuals are asked to summarize their skills and to select the work task dimension areas they wish to use for exploration.

Self-assessment of skills can be very valuable to individuals who are realistic about themselves. It can also be very valuable for individuals who have developed a particular set of work skills and want to apply these to another related occupation. Self-assessment of skills is less useful for an individual who is unrealistic about self or who wants to develop some entirely new skills for a proposed career change.

Measurement of Abilities

In Session 6 of this program, participants took the Career Planning Program (CPP) Ability Tests: Language Usage, Reading Skills, Clerical Skills, Numerical Skills, Mechanical Reasoning, and Space Relations. Research on the relationship between ability test scores and the four work task dimensions has not been conducted. However, common sense applied to definitions of the work tasks—and considered in conjunction with commonly identified types of ability—suggests the relationships shown in Table 2. These relationships also correspond, in a general way, with what is known about persons pursuing occupations whose work tasks are characterized by DATA, IDEAS, PEOPLE, or THINGS.

TABLE 2

Suggested Relationship of Abilities to Basic Work Tasks

Work Tasks	Related Abilities (CPP sections)
DATA	Clerical ability *(Clerical Skills)* Perceptual speed and accuracy Numerical computation *(Numerical Skills)* Eye/hand/finger coordination
IDEAS	Creativity Artistic ability Reading comprehension *(Reading Skills)* Language usage *(Language Usage)* Math Reasoning
PEOPLE	Language skills *(Language Usage)* Social, persuasive, leadership skills (seldom assessed by formal measurement instruments)
THINGS	Mechanical reasoning *(Mechanical Reasoning)* Spatial relations *(Space Relations)* Manual dexterity

From the self-scoring of the CPP Ability Test, participants will get both percentile and stanine scores on each of the six abilities scales. The norm group for these scores is a nationwide group of men and women in technical and community colleges. The percentile score indicates the percentage of individuals in this norm group that scored lower than the person now taking the test. The stanine score is another way of expressing the percentile rank, as indicated in Table 3.

TABLE 3

Stanine Scores and Associated Percentile Ranks

Stanine	Percentile Rank	Verbal Description
9	96-99	Upper 5%
8	89-95	Upper 10%
7	77-88	Upper quarter
6	60-76	
5	40-59	Middle fifth } Middle half
4	23-39	
3	11-22	Lower quarter
2	4-10	Lower 10%
1	1-3	Lower 5%

The six abilities—or skill groups—measured in the test are defined as follows:

- *Mechanical Reasoning:* understanding of how different kinds of mechanical things work. Auto mechanics, engineers, farmers, and lab technicians need mechanical reasoning skills.

- *Numerical Skills:* performing basic mathematical operations: e.g., addition, subtraction, multiplication. Mathematicians and accountants must have good numerical skills. Store clerks and engineering technicians also need some of these skills.

- *Space Relations:* picturing how objects in space would look if seen from different angles. Machinists, artists, architects, and carpenters need this kind of skill.

- *Reading Skills:* reading and understanding different types of material. Most jobs require some reading; certain jobs—such as business executive, lawyer, and scientist—require better reading skills than others. This measure will help judge whether an individual's reading skill is sufficient for the jobs under consideration.

- *Language Usage:* identifying incorrect uses of the English language. Those who can do this will probably avoid mistakes in their own writing. Language usage skills are especially important for secretaries, teachers, editors, and newspaper reporters.

- *Clerical Skills:* ability to follow directions and perform detailed clerical tasks quickly and accurately. These skills are important for file clerks, accountants, secretaries, and computer programmers.

In subsequent versions of this program and of the CPP, the relationship between the scale scores of individuals and the World-of-Work Map will be explained in greater detail than it currently is in the Self-Scoring Answer Folder. For the present, however, individuals should follow the directions on page 8 of the Answer Folder. These directions indicate that the test-taker should find the names of the three scales with the highest stanine scores and check these off wherever they appear in the eight boxes on page 8. Once this is done, the leader should assist individuals to make the following relationship between these eight boxes and the World-of-Work Map regions:

    Box 1: Business Sales & Management = Regions 1 & 2
    Box 2: Business Operations = Regions 3 & 4
    Box 3: Trades, Crafts, Industries = Regions 5 & 6
    Box 4: Technologies = Region 7
    Box 5: Natural & Social Sciences = Region 8
    Box 6: Health Services/Sciences = Region 10 (Family P)
    Box 7: Creative & Applied Arts = Regions 10 & 11
    Box 8: Social & Personal Services = Region 12

Relationships between scale scores and job families can be made by use of the data which follows in Table 4.

In keeping with The American College Testing Program's view that the purpose of testing is to provide focal points for exploration, no specific "cutoff" points are suggested here. In addition, each of these job families contains occupations which utilize a broad range of abilities in the designated areas.

Measured abilities provide an additional focus for occupational exploration. They may be particularly helpful to those whose past work-related experience is limited or to those who cannot assess themselves realistically in a less structured way.

It would be unusual for the assessment of interests, experiences, skills, and abilities to be totally congruent. A congruent picture, however, would serve as strong confirmation of competency and interest in the areas considered.

TABLE 4

Relationship of Ability Scales to Job Families

Job Families	Related CPP Abilities					
	MR	NS	SR	RS	LU	CS
A. Promotion & Direct Contact Sales		X		X	X	
B. Management and Planning		X		X	X	
C. Retail Sales and Service		X		X		X
D. Clerical & Secretarial Work				X	X	X
E. Paying, Receiving, & Bookkeeping		X		X		X
F. Office Machine Operation	X	X		X		X
G. Storage, Dispatching, & Delivery		X		X		X
H. Human Services Crafts		X		X		
I. Repairing & Servicing Equipment	X	X	X	X		
J. Growing and Caring for Plants/Animals		X		X		
K. Construction & Maintenance	X	X	X	X		
L. Transportation Equipment Operator	X	X	X	X		
M. Machine Operating, Servicing, Repair	X	X	X	X		
N. Engineering & Other Applied Tech.	X	X	X	X		
O. Natural Sciences & Mathematics	X	X	X	X	X	
P. Medicine & Medical Technologies	X	X		X		
Q. Social Sciences & Legal Services		X		X	X	
R. Creative Arts	These abilities do not apply.					
S. Applied Arts (Verbal)				X	X	X
T. Applied Arts (Visual)	These abilities do not apply.					
U. Popular Entertainment	These abilities do not apply.					
V. Education and Social Services		X		X	X	
W. Nursing and Human Care	X	X		X		
X. Personal & Household Services		X		X		
Y. Law Enforcement & Protective Services		X		X	X	

MR = Mechanical Reasoning   SR = Space Relations   LU = Language Usage

NS = Numerical Skills   RS = Reading Skills   CS = Clerical Skills

Session 8

Summary

Objective	Suggested Activities	Suggested Time	Materials
1. To raise awareness of the possible effects of stereotyping on vocational choice and career development	Options: A. Guest panel B. Student panel C. Film and discussion	90 minutes	None None "A Different Approach" or some other film

Homework

Read Chapter 8 of the *Career Planning Guide.*

Supplementary Reading

The following magazines:

> *The Black Collegian*
> *Black Enterprise*
> *Mainstream*
> *Women Studies Quarterly*
> *Working Woman*
> *Women's Work*

Resource Material

Film: "A Different Approach," 21 minutes.

> Image Transform
> 4142 Lankershim Blvd.
> W. Hollywood, CA 91602
> (213) 985-7566

Objective and Activities

Objective: To raise awareness of the possible effects of stereotyping on vocational choice and career development

Suggested activities:

Option A—Guest panel. The leader has invited three guests who represent the following groups of possible bias: physically handicapped, career women, racial minorities, and persons in occupations which have traditionally been filled by members of the opposite sex. The guests form a panel and the leader serves as moderator. Some combination of the following questions is used by the moderator to target the panel's discussion:

1. Please introduce yourself briefly, giving your name and your present occupational position.
2. Has your sex, minority group membership, or handicap had any effect upon your work?
3. For those who answer "yes" to the previous question, ask further questions such as:
    a. How did your sex, minority group membership, handicap, etc. affect your original exploration and choice of an occupation?
    b. What kinds of problems did you have in entering or getting through the training or education required for the occupation?
    c. What kinds of problems did you have in securing a position?
    d. What kinds of problems have you had in maintaining the position (work tasks, interpersonal relationships with others, etc.)?
    e. What kinds of problems have you had in receiving promotions, raises, fringe benefits, etc.?
    f. What kinds of things have you done in order to cope with the effects which you have experienced?
    g. Do you have some specific incidents or stories to share with us?
4. For those who said "no," ask:

    What were the factors which minimized the possible effects for you (e.g., occupational field entered; coping skills of the individual; the acceptance of the environment; etc.)
5. This group has been attempting to analyze the internal and external influences on vocational choice and development. In your opinion, are the effects of bias and stereotyping primarily *internal* or *external* factors, or both?
6. With all of the present legislation and emphasis in this area, have you noticed any real change in terms of less stereotyping or greater acceptance?

(**Note:** A copy of the preceding list of questions could be sent to the guest panelists in order to prepare for the class.)

The moderator facilitates communication between participants and the panel, allowing individuals to ask questions. Group participants might be encouraged to volunteer anything they learned from their interviews which either confirms or contradicts what panel members have said.

Suggested time: 90 minutes

Materials: None

Option B—Participant panel. The leader asks for at least three volunteers to act out the roles of the people they interviewed for homework. These individuals become the panel. The discussion is carried out as in Option A above.

Suggested time: 90 minutes

Materials: None

Homework assignment: Read Chapter 8 of the *Career Planning Guide*.

Option C—Film. The film "A Different Approach" is shown, or another selected by the leader. After viewing of the film, the leader stimulates discussion of the content of the film and of its implications for vocational choice and career development.

Session 9

Summary

Objective	Suggested Activities	Suggested Time	Materials/Resources
1. To develop awareness of the external factors which may affect vocational choice and career development	Discussion	20 min.	World-of-Work Map in Appendix A of the *Career Planning Guide*
2. To develop a list of occupations for personal exploration	Completion of back side of World-of-Work Summary Sheet, Appendix A of *Guide*	10 min.	World-of-Work Summary Sheet, Appendix A of *Guide*
3. To learn the process of occupational research	Leader summary of resources listed on the Occupational Research Plan Sheet, Exercise 7	10 min.	Occupational Research Plan Sheet, Exercise 7
4. To learn about local resources for occupational research	Review of materials and systems available (in the local setting) for occupational exploration	60 min.	Access to Career Resource Library (or equivalent); someone to explain materials (if the leader does not do so); demonstration time on computerized system, if available

Homework

Complete Exercise 8—Occupational Research Sheet—for five occupations in Chapter 8 of *Career Planning Guide*.

Resource Materials

Angel, J. L. *Modern Vocational Trends Reference Handbook*. New York: Simon and Schuster, latest edition.

U.S. Department of Labor, United States Employment Service. *Dictionary of Occupational Titles*. Washington, D.C.: U.S. Government Printing Office, latest edition.

Hopke, W. E. *The Encyclopedia of Careers and Vocational Guidance*. Chicago: J. G. Ferguson Publishing Company, latest edition.

Occupational Outlook Handbook. Washington, D.C.: U.S. Government Printing Office, latest edition.

Objectives and Activities

Objective 1: To develop awareness of the external factors which may affect vocational choice and career development

Suggested activities:

A. The leader comments that in Sessions 1-8 an implicit assumption was that an individual can choose freely from any of the 22,000 occupations in the United States. Emphasis was placed upon looking at the self intensively in order to identify personal interests, skills, experiences, and abilities. Each of these self-factors was then used to identify occupations which could utilize them and give the individual a sense of self-actualization. The leader asks participants to think about five people among their family and friends and to consider whether or not these individuals are in their present occupations because they seem to really "fit" in terms of interests, skills, and abilities.

Discussion will probably reveal that some people are fortunate to work in occupations that they really enjoy and in which they feel a very high sense of self-actualization, while others find themselves "trapped" in occupations which do not ideally fit their interests, skills, or experiences. The leader may ask participants why this happens, and discussion should begin to reveal a variety of factors outside the individual which have influenced or dictated the present occupational choice.

B. Participants are asked to think of as many external factors (outside the individual) as possible that may affect the choice of an occupation or the entry into a job. The leader should list these on the board as individuals volunteer them and should ask for a concrete example of how this factor might have an effect. The following factors should be on the longer list that participants might generate:

1. *The general state of the economy* (This affects whether employers are hiring or not.)

2. *Current hiring practices* (If there is a high number of job applicants, employers are able to demand more education and skills than if there is a low number of job applicants for a given occupation.)

3. *Number of applicants available in a given field* (For example, computer programmers have no difficulty getting a good-paying position because there are not enough to fill the demand, while social science teachers are very unlikely to find any openings at all because the need has been over-supplied.)

4. *Current legislation* (For example, a black, female, or handicapped person may have some advantage if a company or institution is attempting to meet a legislated "quota.")

5. *Personal circumstances* (For example, family and financial situations may require that an individual take any job which is available just to earn money to pay for basic needs.)

6. *Opportunity/chance* (Individuals may "fall into" unexpected opportunities.)

C. The leader comments that one of the most important external factors in vocational choice is the job demand or employment outlook in given occupations. In previous sessions the group has looked at the World-of-Work Map in order to relate its occupations to the *internal factors* of interests, skills, and abilities. Now look at the handout to see the percentage of workers (based on the national census) who work in each of the regions (front side) of the World-of-Work Map and in each 2-letter Holland code combination (back side). Process this information with questions like the following:

1. In which of the regions does the job demand appear to be the highest? the lowest?
2. How would you account for this given the current state of the economy, current legislation, or other external factors?
3. What kinds of events could change this distribution of workers significantly?
4. Does this mean that you are assured of a job if you are prepared to enter one of the "high demand" regions?
5. Does it follow that you will not get a job if you are preparing to enter a "low demand" region?
6. What are the two factors which create job openings? (demand for workers in that occupation combined with an undersupply or at least not an oversupply of people trained to enter the occupation)

Suggested time: 20 minutes

Materials: World-of-Work Map in Appendix A of *Career Planning Guide*

Objective 2: To select a list of occupations for personal exploration

Participants are asked to turn to the World-of-Work Summary Sheet in Appendix A of the *Career Planning Guide*. Steps 1 and 2 of the directions on this sheet should have been completed by this time, but the leader should check to make sure that all participants have completed steps 1 and 2. Regions on the map should be marked with I (interests), E (experiences), S (skills), and A (abilities). Also, occupational titles should be filled in for the first four columns on the back of the sheet. At this time, participants should be asked to complete the *fifth column* on the back of the sheet. This fifth column should be a synthesis of the preceding four and should also contain occupational titles which did not show up through any of the four access methods but are of high interest to the students. Some occupations may be eliminated because the participant knows that he or she has no interest in this occupation. On the other hand, occupations which appear in more than one column should be high priority ones for placement in Column 5. Participants should be cautioned not to eliminate occupations about which they have little or no information. In summary, the Column 5 list should be a list of occupations which have high potential for relating to the individual's interests, skills, and abilities and one that the individual is interested in using for the occupational research which follows.

Suggested time: 10 minutes

Materials: World-of-Work Summary Sheet, Appendix A of *Guide*

Objective 3: To learn the process of vocational exploration

Suggested activities:

A. Participants are asked to turn to the Planful Process model in Chapter 2 of the *Career Planning Guide*. The leader points out that the process consists of the following four steps, of which the first three have been accomplished:

Step 1—Identify the decision to be made	= Defining our problem as making a vocational choice and choosing a major.
Step 2—Gather information	= Spending class sessions 3-6 in collecting information about the self, including interests, skills, experiences, and abilities.
Step 3—Identify alternatives	= Relating all of the self-information collected in Step 2 to the World of Work and making the lists on the back of page.
Step 4— Weigh evidence	= Collecting sufficient information about each of the occupations on the list so that it can either be retained as a possibility or discarded.

The course is now at the Step 4 stage, and the remainder of this time period will be spent in acquainting participants with the process of collecting information about occupations and with the resources for doing so.

B. Participants are asked to refer to Exercise 7, the Occupational Research Plan Sheet, of the *Career Planning Guide*. The leader should summarize with the group the four major ways of collecting information about occupations so that evidence can be weighed (Step 4 of the deciding process):

1. *Reading* in the college career resource library or equivalent section of the local public library. The local resources available for this will be reviewed today.

2. *Using computer-based systems, microfiche materials, and/or audiovisual aids.* The local resources available for this will be reviewed today.

3. *Talking directly with individuals* who are in the occupation of interest. This will be an assignment for Session 11.

4. *Finding some ways to "test out" this occupation in real life* (such as work-study, jobs, courses, extracurricular activities).

Participants will be asked to complete this planning summary at the end of this session after being introduced to the local resources for vocational exploration.

Suggested time: 10 minutes

Materials: Occupational Research Plan Sheet, Exercise 7 of *Guide*

Objective 4: To learn about local resources for vocational exploration

(Note: This part of the session will be much more valuable if the group can be taken to the place where vocational exploration resource materials are housed. On a college or university campus, this may be the career planning and placement office, the counseling center, or the library. Noncollege groups might be taken to the public library or to a community counseling center.)

Suggested activities:

A. The group leader, a librarian, or a career specialist or paraprofessional should describe and illustrate all of the resources which fall into the first three categories (printed materials, computer systems and other media, and microfiche systems). This person might ask members of the group to indicate the title of one occupation which they wish to research; some of these titles might be used to illustrate how and where to find information about these occupations.

B. After this orientation to available resource materials, participants are asked to complete the Occupational Research Sheet, Exercise 8 of the *Guide*.

Suggested time: 60 minutes

Materials and resources: Access to Career Resource Library; someone to explain resource; demonstration time on computer-based systems

Homework assignment: Using the resources indicated on the Occupational Research Plan Sheet, thoroughly research *five* occupations from your plan sheet list. Record the information found on the Occupational Research Sheet (Exercise 8).

An Optional Approach to Sessions 10 and 11

As the leader will note from reading the plans for Sessions 10 and 11, the content is very similar. For that reason, depending upon the needs of the group, it may be worthwhile to combine the content of these two sessions into one and to consider one of the following two alternatives for use in the "extra" session:

A. Dismiss one group session, and instead schedule each participant for an individual interview with the group leader or with a career planning counselor, if appropriate. During this interview, group participants would have an opportunity to discuss the findings of assessment instruments used in the program, discuss personal career planning, or ask any questions they might have.

or

B. Allow participants to have this extra time for the planning and carrying out of a final project for this program. This final project should have personal meaning for the individuals, and participants should be encouraged to be creative in the planning of these projects. Some examples:

1. Have one or more job interviews for practice. Write up the experience and report to the group during Session 13 or 14.

2. Talk with one or more personnel managers about the job market in a particular occupational field and about how to get into the field. Write up the experience and report to the group.

3. Talk with recruiting officers about training possibilities for specific occupations in the branches of the military. Write up and report.

4. Talk with two or more individuals in the occupation of the participant's choice. Find out what the career ladder is within the occupation and how promotion takes place. Write up and report.

5. Research graduate schools which offer the training needed for an occupation of the participant's choice. Write up and report.

6. Do detailed research about aspects of government jobs: entry, salary, promotion, employment outlook, etc. Write up and report.

The leader could combine alternatives A and B, thus using the interview as a session for planning the final project.

Session 10
Summary

Objective	Suggested Activities	Suggested Time	Materials
To share occupational information gathered in the homework assignment	Options: A. Reports from group members in panel format B. Reports from group members in dyads C. Guest presenters	100 minutes	Exercise 8, Occupational Research Sheet

Homework

Interview at least one of the two people listed on the Occupational Research Plan Sheet. Use Exercise 9, the Occupational Interview Sheet, for doing so. Be prepared to discuss this interview in the next class session.

Objective and Activities

Objective: To share occupational information gathered in the homework assignment

Suggested activities:

Option A. Reports from group members in panel format

The leader writes the titles for four columns on the board: IDEAS, DATA, PEOPLE, and THINGS; and then asks participants to name one of the five occupations they researched in depth. These titles are listed under the appropriate column on the board. Participants are asked to sit together according to the column in which their occupation falls: e.g., those with occupations that primarily involve people would sit together. Members of each group present their occupational reports to the total group, moderated by the leader. The leader should encourage those in the nonreporting groups to ask questions, perhaps using the Occupational Research Sheet as a guide. This exercise can be repeated several times with the students' other occupations, if time allows. If this is done, ask students to physically move to the work task area of their next occupation.

After hearing the reports of occupations in one work task area, participants should discuss the similarities between these occupations. Referring to the World-of-Work Map in Appendix A of the *Career Planning Guide,* ask participants to find the Job Family of the occupation just reported. A Job Family includes a number of occupations that involve similar work activities. Having access to these related occupations can be useful for a number of reasons:

1. If the occupation you researched turns out to be the "wrong" one for you, you can refer to other occupational titles in your Job Family. Specific titles are listed in the Job Family Charts in Appendix A of the *Career Planning Guide.*

2. You can also consider Job Families closest to your Job Family and find titles of occupations for these families on the chart. These occupations would also involve similar work tasks.

3. The occupations listed on the chart are the most common ones. A counselor could help you to develop a more extensive list.

(Note to leader: These points should help the students understand the importance of considering related occupations and allow them to recognize their flexibility in moving from one occupation to another.)

Option B. Reports from group members in dyads

The leader asks participants to break up into dyads. One member of the dyad serves as interviewer, and the other plays the role of person in the occupation. The interviewer uses the Occupational Research Sheet as a basis for the interview questions. The interviewee, responding as a person in one of the five occupations researched, answers in the first person. When one interview has been completed, the members of the dyad reverse roles. This process can continue with the formation of new sets of dyads. The leader may process this experience with the total group with some general questions of this nature:

1. What did you learn about some occupations that surprised you most?

2. What occupations appear to have positive employment outlooks? Which seem to be declining?

3. What relationship, if any, did you find between educational entry level and income?

4. What relationship, if any, did you find between a value of helping others and income?

5. Which occupations, if any, did you find that have a more serious impact on other life roles than others? Why?

6. Which occupations did you research that allow you to work primarily with data? with people? with ideas? with things? (The leader might "plot" these occupations on a World-of-Work Map which has been drawn on the board or a flip chart.)

7. What else do you need to learn about these occupations in order to make a good decision about entering them?

Option C. Guest presenters

The leader, (with the assistance of group participants, local service organizations, alumni, etc.) may invite a panel of 4-8 people in to represent the dimensions of the World-of-Work Map. These individuals should be selected on the basis of their representation of occupational fields in the four work task dimensions that members of the group might have interest in entering. They should also represent occupations that are rather "pure" in the four dimensions, so that comparisons can be clearly made in regard to work tasks and work settings. Examples:

DATA: accountant, claims adjuster, bookkeeper, legal secretary

PEOPLE: teacher, counselor, occupational therapist, nurse, personnel worker, salesperson

THINGS: engineer, computer programmer, engineer technician, drafter

IDEAS: commercial artist, photographer, medical doctor, audiologist

The leader should serve as moderator of the panel and provide some structured questions relating to work tasks, work settings, employment outlook, methods of entering the field, educational training needed, and degree of orientation to working with data, people, things, and ideas. The leader should also "field" questions from the class participants for the speakers.

Suggested time: 100 minutes

Materials: Exercise 8, Occupational Research Sheet, in Chapter 8 of the *Guide*

Homework assignment: Interview at least one of the two people listed on your Occupational Research Plan Sheet using the Occupational Interview Sheet, Exercise 9 in the *Guide*. If possible, conduct this interview in the actual work setting. Upon completion of the interview,

1. Write it up in the form suggested on the Interview Sheet. Be prepared to discuss the interview in next week's session and to hand in the written report.

    or

    Tape the interview so that it can be listened to in next week's session.

2. Photograph the individual and his or her work setting for presentation in next week's session.

    or

    Bring the individual to the next session for interview in front of the group.

Session 11

Summary

Objective	Suggested Activities	Suggested Time	Materials
To experience the process of interviewing a person in a selected occupation	Options: A. Participant panel B. Guest panel C. Field trip D. Audiovisual presentation	100 minutes	Exercise 9, Occupational Interview Sheet

Homework

Work on final projects.

Supplementary Reading

Terkel, Studs. *Working: People Talk About What They Do All Day and How They Feel About What They Do.* New York: Pantheon Books, 1972.

Objective and Activities

Objective: To experience the process of interviewing people in a variety of occupations

Suggested activities:

Option A. Participant panel

1. The leader asks participants to indicate the occupation of the person whom they have interviewed. These occupational titles are placed on the board or a flip chart. Participants are asked to select four occupations that they want to hear about first. The four individuals are asked to form a panel in the front of the room and to play the part of the people in the four occupations. Participants are invited to direct any questions they choose to one member or all members of the panel. If participants need prodding, some key questions are:

    a. What does a person do in your occupation? (or: What do you do every day?)

    b. How much training is needed to do what you do? Is that training difficult to get into?

    c. Is special licensing or certification needed?

    d. What is the salary range in your occupation?

    e. How did you get into your occupation?

    f. If you were promoted, where could you be promoted to?

g. Are there plenty of jobs in your field?

h. What is the typical way of getting into your work?

i. What effect does your occupation have on the way you live, where you live, the friends you have, or your family responsibilities?

j. What are some of the *most* desirable things about your occupation? some of the *least* desirable?

k. Could your job be in jeopardy because of economic conditions or changing technology?

l. If you could decide all over again, would you go into this occupation?

m. What advice do you have for someone who is thinking about entering your occupation?

2. The group leader summarizes the responses given by the members of the panel by pointing out similarities and differences among the occupations and highlighting any particularly relevant information.

3. The group selects another panel of four occupational representatives and repeats the process suggested in "1." This process continues as long as time allows.

Option B. Guest panel

A panel of guests, brought in by group participants, is interviewed, using the questions on the Occupational Interview Sheet (Exercise 9 of *Guide*) and any others generated by the group.

Option C. Field trip to work setting

By prearrangement the group goes to an industry, business, institution, or agency which offers a wide variety of occupations. Selected employees come to a conference room to be interviewed by members of the group in front of the whole group. This might be combined or replaced by a tour of the organization or company during which participants are encouraged to ask questions of workers.

Option D. Audiovisual presentation

If a significant number of group members have elected to present their occupational research in the form of taped interviews or pictures of interviewees on the job, a part of the session time could be used to hear and see these presentations. Group members may ask additional questions of the presenters.

For each of the options the group leader can conclude with discussion based on the following questions:

1. After all the research you have done on the occupations of your choice, what else do you need to do in order to make a good decision about entering this occupation?

2. How would you go about taking these next steps or acquiring additional information?

3. What kinds of inconsistencies did you find in the information you acquired? How can you resolve them?

4. If you decided to enter one of the occupations you are researching, what would be your entry position and what would the career ladder in this occupation be?

Suggested time: 100 minutes

Materials: Exercise 9, Occupational Interview Sheet

Homework assignment: Work on final projects.

Session 12
Summary

Objective	Suggested Activities	Suggested Time	Materials
1. To provide orientation to the narrowing process	Mini-lecture	10 min.	None
2. To become aware of some important job characteristics and their implications	Group discussion of job characteristics & related occupations	20 min.	None
3. To provide an introduction to work values	Mini-lecture and discussion of values in general	10 min.	None
	Object-of-value exercise	15 min.	None
	Mini-lecture on Katz's values	15 min.	pages 95 to 96 of this manual
	Values Auction	30 min.	Values Auction instruction sheet (one for each participant), in Appendix A of this manual

Homework

Read Chapters 9 and 10 of *Guide*.

Complete Exercise 10, Preferred Job Characteristics and Values.

Supplementary Reading

Katz, Martin R. *Decisions and Values*. New York: College Entrance Examination Board, 1963.

Katz, Martin R. "A Model of Guidance for Career Decision-Making." *Vocational Guidance Quarterly, 15,* No. 1 (1966), 2-10.

Objectives and Activities

Objective 1: To provide orientation to the narrowing process

Suggested activity: Introductory mini-lecture

The group leader reviews the Planful Decision-making Model again and indicates that the members of the group are at Step 5 of the process, that is, making choice(s). In the early stages of the vocational exploration and deciding process, the group participated in a number of activities (such as exploration by interests, skills, experiences, and abilitites) designed to *increase* the number of vocational alternatives considered. In this later stage of the deciding process, it is necessary to *decrease* alternatives. This is done by "weighing" each alternative in the light of *internal* factors possessed and *external* factors desired or imposed. In today's session, attention will be given to two "narrowers": job characteristics and work values. After this introduction, group members will use these narrowers in the assignment for the next session: to reduce the number of occupations under consideration and to put them in priority order (as called for in steps 4 and 5 of the Planful process).

Suggested time: 10 minutes

Materials: None

Objective 2: To become aware of some important job characteristics and their implications

Suggested activity: Group discussion

The leader asks the group to think about characteristics which vary from occupation to occupation. As individuals suggest these, they may be listed on a board or flip chart. The list should include at least the following:

- Amount of education or training needed to enter the occupation
- Income
- Number of job openings (future outlook or demand)
- Work setting (i.e., indoors in an office, laboratory, or hospital; outdoors; some combination of indoor and outdoor)
- Work tasks (i.e., working with data, people, things, ideas)
- Work hours
- Travel as a part of the work
- Level of responsibility
- Degree of physical danger involved
- Degree of physical activity involved

After the list of characteristics is completed, the leader asks members of the group to divide into subgroups of 5 or 6 individuals. The leader then gives one of the following combinations of characteristics to each group. Each group has two assignments: (a) to think of three occupations that would combine these characteristics, and (b) to think about the implications for the lifestyle of a person who is in an occupation with these characteristics.

Group 1:

- Income of $40,000 per year
- High level of responsibility
- Little physical activity involved
- Work in an office
- Irregular work hours

Group 2:
- Income of $15,000—$20,000
- A lot of local travel
- A lot of physical danger
- Regular work hours
- Work inside and outside

Group 3:
- High degree of physical activity
- Irregular work hours
- Low level of responsibility
- Working with tools or equipment
- Income of $10,000—$15,000

Group 4:
- Graduate work needed for entry
- Very tight job market
- Work indoors
- High level of responsibility
- Working with people

Suggested time: 20 minutes

Materials: None

Objective 3: To provide an introduction to work values

Suggested activities:

A. Mini-lecture and discussion

The leader indicates that job characteristics are *external* factors which relate to occupations although they do have effects on personal lifestyle. Values, on the other hand, are factors *internal* to an individual. Ideally, an occupation provides an opportunity for individuals to have their personal value system fulfilled. The leader stimulates discussion with questions such as:

1. What is a *value?*

    The leader should bring the group to the conclusion that a value is "a belief held strongly enough that an individual can put it into words, is willing to tell other people about it, and is willing to accept it as a guide to action and decision making."

2. What are some general life values?

   Expect answers like: family, nature, religious beliefs, prestige, money, freedom, etc.

B. Object-of-value exercise

The leader puts the group in a circle and asks each individual to lay on the table or desk the most important item he or she is carrying in a pocket, purse, wallet, or bag. The leader then asks each person to:

1. Tell others what the object is;

2. Explain why it is important; and

3. Name the value expressed by it.

C. Mini-lecture on Katz's ten work values

The leader presents Katz's ten work-related values (see pages 95-96 of this manual), explains each and gives examples (or asks others to give examples) of occupations which provide a high potential for meeting each of these values.

D. The Values Auction

The leader passes out the Values Auction and reviews the values as defined on the instruction sheet. The leader also reviews the following rules for the auction:

1. Each person has $500 to spend at the auction.

2. Each of the values has a minimum price of $100; that is, bids will begin at $100.

3. Bids must be placed in increments of $10; in others words, a given bidder cannot raise the price which is on the floor more than $10.

4. After each value is "bought," the leader will write the name of the value, its final price, and the name of its owner on the board.

The leader conducts the values auction and writes the names of values, owners, and final prices on the board. When the auction is completed, it is summarized with these questions:

1. How did you feel when you couldn't get a value which you wanted?

2. Were you satisfied with the values you were able to get?

3. Did the exercise help you to clarify or place relative importance on your values?

4. How much were you willing to put yourself on the line for what you felt was important?

Suggested time: 70 minutes

Materials: Instruction Sheet for Values Auction (master copy in Appendix A of this manual)

Homework assignment: Read Chapters 9 and 10 of the *Guide*.

  Complete Exercise 10, Preferred Job Characteristics and Values.

Background

Rationale for Placement of Job Characteristics and Work Values

In the earlier sessions of this program (Sessions 4-7), emphasis was placed upon factors which are *internal* to the individual—interests, skills, experiences, and abilities. These factors were used to assist individuals to identify occupations for detailed exploration, that is, to find some plot point for exploration in the World of Work. It was hoped by the authors that these sessions and experiences would have a broadening effect upon participants' perception of available options and would create an extensive list of possible occupational alternatives. Research in the field of career development supports the use of these internal factors as the most valid ones for occupational choice and satisfaction.

In the sequential process of vocational choice, there is, however, a time to expand options and then a time to narrow options, discarding some based upon information collected and preferences identified. The purpose of this session, then, is to provide two "narrowers," work values and job characteristics. In Exercise 10, assigned for Session 13, participants are asked to express preferences related to ten work values and six job characteristics. These stated preferences are then used to help reduce and prioritize the list of occupations under consideration.

Work Values

This session focuses on ten work values identified through years of research by Dr. Martin Katz and his colleagues at the Educational Testing Service. Katz defines these ten values as follows:

1. *High income.* Some minimum income (enough for survival) is essential for everyone. But beyond that, how important to you are the extras? People have different ideas about how much income is "high." Therefore, high income is not defined here as a specific amount. It means more than enough to live on. It means money to use as you wish after you have paid your basic living expenses.

2. *Prestige.* If people respect you, look up to you, listen to your opinions, or seek your help in community affairs, you are a person with prestige. Of course, prestige can be gained in several ways. But in present-day America, occupation is usually the key to prestige. Rightly or wrongly, we respect some occupations more than others.

3. *Independence.* Some occupations give you more freedom than others to make your own decisions, to work without supervision or direction from others. At one extreme might be talented free-lance artists or writers who may work without any supervision. At the other extreme might be military service or some big business organizations with chains of command which severely limit the decisions each person can make.

4. *Helping others.* Most people are willing to help others and show it every day outside of their work. They put themselves out to do favors, make gifts, donate to charities, and so on. This does not count here. The question here is: Do you want helping others to be a *main part* of your occupation? To what extent do you want to devote your life work directly to helping people improve their health, education, or welfare?

5. *Security.* In the most secure occupations, you will be free from the fear of losing your job and income. You will have tenure—that is, you cannot be fired very easily. Employment

will tend to remain high in spite of recessions, and there will be no seasonal ups and downs. Your income will generally remain stable and predictable; it will not vanish with hard times. Your occupation is not likely to be wiped out by automation or other technological changes.

6. *Variety.* Occupations with the greatest variety offer many different kinds of activities and problems, frequent changes in location, new people to meet. Variety is the opposite of routine, predictability, or repetition. If you value variety highly, you probably like novelty and surprise, and enjoy facing new problems, events, places and people.

7. *Leisure.* How important is the amount of time your occupation will allow you to spend away from work? Leisure may include short hours, long vacations, or the chance to choose your own time off. To place high value on leisure is like saying, "The satisfactions I get away from the job are so important to me that work must not interfere with them."

8. *Leadership.* Do you want to guide others, tell them what to do, be responsible for their performance? People who rank leadership high usually want power to control events. They want to influence people to work together effectively. They are willing to accept the blame when things go wrong, even though they were not at fault.

9. *Early entry.* How important is it to you to enter an occupation right away? You can enter some occupations with very little education or training. Other occupations require years of expensive education, which delay your entry into the occupation. If early entry is important to you, this means you would not be willing to put up with a long period of education or training. If you are willing to delay entering an occupation and to go through additional years of education and training, then early entry is less important to you.

10. *Work in main field of interest.* Some people have only one main field of interest (scientific, technological, administrative, personal contact, verbal, or aesthetic); others are interested in two or more of these fields. Some insist that their occupation must be in one of their major fields of interest. Others are willing to work in a field that is less interesting; they feel they can satisfy their main interest in their spare time.[3]

Since these definitions are very general ones, more specific designations of a high, medium, or low level of each of these values may be useful. The following table provides more specific definitions of each of three levels. These definitions were developed by the DISCOVER Foundation for use in its computerized system, DISCOVER.

---

[3] Adapted from the System for Interactive Guidance and Information (SIGI). Copyright 1972 and 1974 by the Educational Testing Service. All rights reserved. Reproduced by permission.

TABLE 5

Values and Operational Definitions by Rating Level

VALUE	Level 1	Level 2	Level 3
High Income	Under $15,000	$15,000-$30,000	$30,000 and up
Prestige	Occupations which have been considered menial in our society	Occupations to which society attributes a medium level of prestige	Occupations which society "looks up to"
Independence	Occupations in which work tasks and schedule are usually under close supervision	Occupations which allow the worker some flexibility in planning work tasks and schedule	Occupations in which individuals usually or almost always plan their own work tasks and schedule
Helping Others	Occupations in which there is little or no involvement with others' physical, emotional or educational well-being	Occupations in which some activity is directed toward others' physical, emotional, or educational well-being	Occupations in which the major thrust of activity is for others' physical, emotional or educational well-being
Security	Occupations in which individuals may easily lose their positions due to economic conditions	Occupations which have no built-in tenure system, but also are not easily subject to factors such as economic conditions or seasonality	Occupations in which, due to built-in tenure systems, individuals very seldom lose their positions
Variety	Occupations which are characterized by routine tasks	Occupations which provide some variety of work tasks	Occupations which offer a wide variety of work tasks, sometimes coupled with a variety of work settings and kinds of people to work with
Leadership	Occupations which provide no opportunity for leadership	Occupations which may provide some opportunity for leadership, but seldom of more than 25 people	Occupations in which an individual leads, supervises, or influences at least 25 people
Leisure	Occupations in which one may be called upon to work at any hour on any day of the week and/or customarily to take work home	Occupations in which one may be expected to work irregular hours or weekends, and/or to take work home occasionally	Occupations in which one almost always works normal hours between 8:00 and 5:00 and never takes work home
Early Entry	Occupations which require more than four years of college for entry	Occupations which require education beyond high school up to and including four years of college	Occupations which can be entered immediately after high school or without completing high school

Source: DISCOVER Foundation, Inc. Copyright 1976. Used by permission.

Note. The tenth value—"Field of Interest"—is not covered here.

Job Characteristics

In this session and in the homework assignment of Session 13, both work values and job characteristics have been used. There is a very high degree of overlap between the two. The job characteristic of regular vs. irregular work hours has a high degree of relationship to the personal value of *leisure*. The job characteristic of increasing job demand vs. declining or stable demand has a high degree of relationship to the personal value of *security*. For these reasons, it is difficult to make clean breaks between work values and job characteristics. In the assignment for Session 13, participants will evaluate each of the occupations on their lists in light of the following values and characteristics:

Katz Values	**Job Characteristics**
Entry Level	Job Availability
Income Level	Work Setting
Field of Interest	Work Tasks
Leisure	Work Hours
Variety	Travel
Leadership	Level of Responsibility (related to Independence)
Prestige	Physical Danger
Security	Physical Activity

Session 13
Summary

Objective	Suggested Activities	Suggested Time	Materials
1. To identify a major or program of study related to vocational choice or interest	Exercise 12, Programs/Majors Indexed by ACT Job Family	10 min.	Exercise 12, Programs/Majors Indexed by ACT Job Family
2. To complete and discuss the Career Action Plan	Complete Exercise 11, Personal Career Action Plan	30 min.	Exercise 11, Personal Career Action Plan
3. To provide instruction on resume writing	Mini-lecture Complete Exercise 13, Standard Resume Worksheet, and/or Exercise 14, Functional Resume Worksheet	40 min.	Exercise 13, Standard Resume Worksheet Exercise 14, Functional Resume Worksheet
4. To plan major project (or to make reports to class if projects were assigned in Session 11)	Plan individualized assignments or give oral reports on projects already completed.	20 min.	None

Homework

Prepare to give oral report to class on individual project. Write up project to hand in.

Supplementary Readings (for leader or participants)

Ballard, J. *How to Get to Do What You've Always Wanted to Do . . . And Get Paid for Doing It? Why Not?* Amherst, Mass.: Mandale, 1976.

Bolles, R. N. *What Color Is Your Parachute?* Berkeley: Ten Speed Press, 1979.

Bostwick, B. E. *Finding the Job You've Always Wanted* (2nd edition). New York: John Wiley and Sons, Inc., 1979.

Carkhuff, R. R. *Get a Job.* Amherst, Mass.: Human Resource Development Press, 1975.

Crystal, J. & Bolles, R. N. *Where Do I Go From Here With My Life?* Berkeley: Ten Speed Press, 1978.

Irish, R. K. *Go Hire Yourself an Employer.* Garden City, N.Y.: Doubleday & Co., Inc., 1978.

Jackson, T. & Mayleas, D. *The Hidden Job Market.* New York: Quadrangle Books, 1976.

Lewis, A. *How to Write Better Resumes.* Woodbury, N.Y.: Barrons' Educational Series, Inc., 1975.

Strohmenger, C. T. *How to Complete Job Application Forms.* Falls Church, Va.: American Personnel & Guidance Association, 1975.

Resource Materials

Films: "Job Hunt," AIMS Instructional Media, Inc., 626 Justin Ave., Glendale, CA 91201.

"Communicating Effectively," Barr Films, 34902 Foothill Blvd., Pasadena, CA 91107.

Videotape: "Career Development," Video Series, hosted by Richard Bolles.

Objectives and Activities

Objective 1: To identify a major or program of study related to vocational choice or interest

Suggested activities:

A. Ask participants to identify the job family of occupations of highest interest, using the charts in Appendix B of the *Career Planning Guide*. Once the job family is identified, turn to Exercise 12 of the *Guide* to identify majors and/or vocational-technical programs of study.

and/or

B. Using the information gained about high-priority occupations through reading, interviewing, computers, and media (see Exercise 7, item 2), identify a program of study needed for entry with selected occupations.

Suggested time: 10 minutes

Materials: Exercise 12, Programs/Majors Indexed by ACT Job Family

Objective 2: To complete and discuss the Career Action Plan

Suggested activity:

The group leader asks participants to complete the Personal Career Action Plan in Chapter 10 of the *Guide*. After all have completed this summary, the leader asks each group member to share the plans indicated on the sheet. Group members are encouraged to ask questions of individuals, and the leader serves as active facilitator.

Suggested time: 30 minutes

Materials: Exercise 11, Personal Career Action Plan

Objective 3: To provide instruction on resume writing

Suggested activity: mini-lecture on resume writing

Although not all students are ready to enter the job market, all will eventually do so; to do this, resume and cover letter writing are vital skills. The leader uses the "Background" information to provide instruction on the writing of cover letters and resumes. Participants are referred to Chapter 10 of the *Guide*, which provides sample letters and resumes as well as instructions for writing them. At this time the leader asks participants to complete Exercise 13, the Standard Resume Worksheet, and Exercise 14, the Functional Resume Worksheet.

Objective 4: To plan major project (or to begin to make reports to class if these were assigned in Session 11)

Suggested activity:

The purpose of this part of the session is to plan an individualized assignment for each participant for next week. Based upon the plans reported from the Career Action Plan, make assignments like the following:

Still undecided about choice and occupation: Do additional research and write it up.

Still undecided about major or program of study: Talk to appropriate people (counselors, advisers, department heads, etc.) and write a report.

Plan to transfer to another undergraduate institution or to graduate school: Use resources (reference books or computers) to do research. Write this up indicating possible choice of next school.

Planning to go to the job market: Polish and type the resume and cover letter begun in the class session or have some practice job interviews.

Planning to go to military or apprenticeship: Visit appropriate persons (recruiting offices or apprenticeship office), and write it up.

Planning to be in the same institution next year: Plan choice of study appropriate for vocational choice. Talk to adviser about selection of courses. Write this up.

Reading one or more of the books listed under "Supplementary Reading," Session 13.

Resources for participants are found following Exercise 12 in the *Career Planning Guide*

Suggested time: 20 minutes for planning; additional time as needed for reports

Materials: None

Homework assignment: Prepare to give oral report on final project. Write up report to hand in.

Background

Courses and Post-High School Educational Programs/Majors Indexed by ACT Job Family

If the Personal Life and Career Planning Program is being taught as a college course, one of the significant decisions students have to make is the choice of a major. A tool developed by The American College Testing Program to assist students to explore majors constitutes Exercise 12 of the *Career Planning Guide*. In this chart, high school course areas, one-year and two-year post-high school programs/majors, and four-year college majors have been related to the 25 job families. This relationship was accomplished by looking at the typical work tasks, academic preparation, and skills required in each job family and relating these to educational programs and majors.

The chart can be used for two purposes: (1) to identify a job family or families (and therefore specific occupations) in which a given major can be used, and (2) to find out which major or program of specialty would be related to a given occupation or group of occupations. This chart is meant to be an exploratory tool. Once exploration is focused, individuals need to read reliable occupational information to obtain a higher level of detail about the requirements for entry into a specific occupation. Since a job family includes a variety of related occupations, the specific training required will vary from one occupation to another within any given job family.

Resume Writing

The outline for this session suggests that the leader provide a short lecture on the preparation of a resume. There are many excellent publications that address this topic, and many colleges and agencies have their own publications. It is strongly suggested that the leader utilize the latest material in the field to prepare for this presentation. The suggestions which follow are provided to help the leader structure the material to be presented. Other publications may help to fill in important details.

Suggested Outline for Presentation on Resume Writing
(included as "Guidelines for Resume Writing" in Chapter 10 of *Guide*)

1. Purposes in writing a resume

   a. To assist the individual to formulate a clear picture of career goals and competencies.

   b. To present to prospective employers a concise self-picture that is attractive enough to secure an interview. Unless the candidate can convince the prospective employer to spend the time on an interview, it is impossible to get the position.

2. Contents of a resume

   a. There is no *one* correct list of items which must be included in every resume. The following is an acceptable list from which to choose:

      - Name, address, phone number(s).

      - *Career objective*—If the resume is to be used for a variety of jobs, it might be better to include this in the cover letter.

      - *Education*—Begin with latest degree and move chronologically backward; high school experience is usually not included.

      - *Honors*—If there are any significant ones to report.

      - *Work experience*—Begin with latest job and move chronologically backward.

      - *Activities and Interests*

      - *References*—This can be handled with the sentence "References will be furnished upon request." Names of individuals are not usually listed on the resume.

   b. Do *not* include anything in the resume which is negative or can be interpreted by an employer as negative:

      - Grade point average: 1.3

      - Marital status: divorced

- Height and weight: 5′ 2″, 180 lbs.
- Extracurricular/leisure activities: none

c. Put all the content in the most positive light possible. For example:

Instead of . . .	Say . . .
"Stocked shelves in dime store"	"Had experience in merchandise display in a large chain store"
"Had to listen to compliants of customers"	"Gained valuable experience in relating to the public"
"Hope to finally make manager some day"	"Plan to reach the managerial level within five years"

3. Format of the resume

   a. There is no *one* correct format for the resume. The writer may use some degree of originality in presenting his or her self-picture. The two common most forms—the *standard resume* and the *functional resume*—are illustrated in the *Career Planning Guide*.

   Rather than simply providing a list of experiences, the functional resume attempts to describe and document *skills possessed*. It is often longer, and makes use of first-person pronouns and complete descriptive sentences.

   b. The appearance of the resume must be impeccable.

      1. It should be concise, not more than one to one and half pages in length.
      2. It must be *typed*. Good copies of a typed original are totally acceptable.
      3. Spelling, punctuation, and grammar must be perfect.
      4. Format and appearance must be attractive.

4. Use of the resume

   The resume is usually mailed to a prospective employer along with a cover letter. It may be sent either to apply for a job which is currently open or to be kept on file in case a job does open. Sometimes a resume is hand-carried to a prospective employer at the time of an interview.

Standard Resume Worksheet
(included in *Career Planning Guide*)

Name:

Address (include city, state, and zip code—spell out in full):

Telephone numbers (include area code):

Career objective (not more than two sentences):

Education:

Work experience:

Interests and activities (if desired):

Personal information:

References: Furnished upon request

Functional Resume Worksheet
(included in *Career Planning Guide*)

Name

Address

(Include city, state, and zip code; spell out in full.)

Telephone number

(Include area code.)

Career objective

(Limit this to about two sentences and use *skill words* to describe your ideal job specifications—for example, "a responsible, administrative position using demonstrated skills in . . ." Then list your strongest skills.)

Summary of experience

Job title (use a transferrable skill word instead of job title), company, city, state, dates worked (optional)

Areas of effectiveness

(*Use skill words in "ING" form. Use the lines below to describe **in detail**—three or four sentences— where and how you used each of these skills. Give two or three examples of your use of each skill from your past working experience, whether volunteer, full-time, or part-time.)

*Skill word or phrase _____

_____

_____

_____

*Skill word or phrase _____

_____

_____

_____

*Skill word or phrase _____

_____

_____

_____

*Skill word or phrase _____

_____

_____

_____

Education

Name of school, city, state, dates (optional)

Special knowledge

Session 14
Summary

Objective	Suggested Activities	Suggested Time	Materials
1. To hear remaining project summaries	Oral reports on projects	30 min. (or more if needed)	Final projects
2. To provide a futuristic summary experience	Future Fantasy	20 min.	Career Fantasy, pages 109-111 of this manual
3. To share final feedback on course experience	Sentence Stems and/or Locally-developed evaluation questionnaires	20 min.	Locally-developed questionnaires (optional)
4. To clarify cognitive material from the program	Review session	20 min.	None
5. To evaluate course effectiveness	Post-test evaluation instruments	30 min.	Same instrument used in Session 1 and answer sheets (one set for each participant) Pencils

Objectives and Activities

Objective 1: To hear remaining project summaries

Depending upon the time at which projects were assigned, the number of participants in the group, and how many reports have already been given, additional time may be needed in this session for oral reports on the projects undertaken in Session 10 or 13. As much time as is needed to complete these reports should be taken, with consideration of the other objectives which the leader wants to accomplish in this session.

Suggested time: Variable

Materials: Final projects of participants

and/or

Objective 2: To provide a futuristic summary experience

Suggested activity: *Career Fantasy*

The leader introduces the activity by indicating that the purpose of this session is to sum up the experiences of this program. This will be done by means of a Career Fantasy. Ask participants to close their eyes and relax. Read the Career Fantasy on the following pages, asking the group to allow their imaginations to fill in all of the information which they have been able to get from this program. When reading is completed, ask volunteers to describe the fantasy which they have just had. Discussion questions like the following can be used:

1. How easy was it for you to imagine yourselves ten years from now?

2. How realistic or obtainable do you feel your fantasies were?

3. In your fantasy were you playing the same roles on the Life-Career Rainbow that you chose in Session 3 in the Life-Career Rainbow exercise?

4. Which roles were most important to you? Which, if any, conflicted?

5. In your fantasy, did the occupation which you have now tentatively selected seem to "fit" with your total career?

Suggested time: 30 minutes

Materials: Career Fantasy, pages 109-111 of this manual

and/or

Objective 3: To share final feedback on program experience

Suggested activities:

A. *Sentence stems.*

The leader introduces the activity by asking participants to share their reactions, impressions, and feelings about the program and their own progress in the career decision-making process.

The leader lists the following sentence stems on the board or on a flip chart:

> I learned that . . .
> I was pleased that . . .
> I was displeased that . . .
> I wonder how . . .
> I wonder if . . .
> I wonder when . . .
> I expect that . . .
> I wish that . . .
> I hope that . . .
> I was disappointed that . . .

Each participant selects any sentence stem he or she wishes and completes the statement. Try to help students focus on personal knowledge acquired rather than on generalized statements: e.g., "I learned that **I**" rather than "I learned that people." Each person must complete *at least one* sentence stem.

B. Any locally-developed evaluation questionnaires may be completed at this time.

Suggested time: 20 minutes

Materials: Locally-developed evaluation questionnaires (optional)

and/or

Objective 4: To clarify cognitive material from the program

Review session—In preparation for the exam (if one is developed by the leader) the leader invites any questions that participants may have about material covered in the program. The leader may also structure a review session and suggest a list of topics which should be studied again.

Suggested time: 20 minutes

Materials: None

and/or

Objective 5: To evaluate course effectiveness

Post-test evaluation instruments. Leader administers the evaluation instrument again, stating the purposes for using these materials (refer to Session 1, Objective 1).

Suggested time: 30 minutes

Materials: One evaluation instrument and answer sheet for each participant
 Pencils

Career Fantasy

Instructions: I want you to relax, close your eyes if you wish, and get involved in a bit of fantasy. Imagine that you are ten years older than you are today. It is a weekday, and I want you to imagine one that is exactly the way you would like it to be. Ready to begin?

It's morning, and you're getting up. What time is it?

You begin to get dressed for whatever you are going to do today. What are you putting on: jeans? a business suit or dress? informal sports clothes? a uniform of some kind?

You might be heading for breakfast now. With whom are you living: a husband? a wife? a friend? by yourself? with dogs and goldfish? other members of a specially-planned community? Do you have responsibility to take care of or help any of these people you live with before you begin your day's activities?

What are you doing next? Do you leave the house to do some work tasks or do you stay at home? If you leave the house, how far do you have to travel? And how do you get there: by car (Mercedes, Datsun, Ford), by bus, by subway, by bicycle, on foot . . . or do you fly to some distant place today?

Now that you are ready to begin your work tasks, what time is it? Are you expected to begin your work at the same time every day? Or are you allowed to have some variation in your schedule?

What is your place of work like? Are you inside or outside? If you are inside, are you at home, in an office, a factory, a laboratory, a school, a hospital, an airplane? If you are outside, are you at a construction site, on a farm, on a body of water, in a forest? Do you have some work inside and some outside? Are you moving from place to place as you work? Is it hot, cold, smelly, dirty, air-conditioned, neat, plush, casual? Do you work in the same place every day?

In your work today, are you working with *people:* to teach them, help them, counsel them, manage them, lead them, sell them something? Or are you working with *things:* like tools, equipment, machines, products? Are you making something, repairing it, designing it, testing it?

Are you working with *ideas:* to undertand some phenomenon of nature? to test out a new theory? to create a new piece of art or music? Are you working with *data* (facts, numbers, information): to organize records, to collect new information? to draw some conclusions from information? or to present it in some new way?

Does your work require a lot of mental activity? Does it require physicial activity? Do you sit most of the time? or stand? or are you exerting a lot of physical energy?

Did it take a lot of education or training to get your job? Did you complete college, go to graduate school, take special technical training? Will more education be required periodically to keep yourself up to date?

Are you doing the same thing today that you did yesterday and will do tomorrow? Or is today quite different from yesterday? May this afternoon provide some new challenge?

Are you working by yourself? Are you working by yourself but side by side with others? Are you working directly with people?

Is someone supervising you very closely or to some degree? Or are *you* deciding what you will do next? Are you working for yourself or for someone else?

Now it's time for lunch. Did you bring a bag lunch? Are you eating with the people you work with? Are you going out for a fast lunch? Or don't you have time for lunch today at all? Are you taking a customer or client out to a nice restaurant? Do you have 28 minutes for lunch, an hour, or can you take as long as you want?

Now that you have returned from lunch, what are you doing this afternoon? Are your tasks the same as this morning? Are you looking at the clock to see if it's almost time to go home, or to find out if you can possibly finish all the work you want to finish before you go home?

Do you get paid today? How big is your check? Do you get paid on a regular basis or whenever a particular piece of work is finished? Do you get the same amount every time you are paid, or do you get a variable amount depending upon the commissions or tips you've earned or how good business was this month? Or don't you get paid at all? What has been taken out of your check—insurance payments, money to purchase stocks in the company? Or does the company pay the insurance and help you purchase the stocks?

Do you have a good chance of keeping this job for a long time? Or are you concerned about losing it because the product or service you provide is being needed less and less? Are there more and more young people entering the occupation? Do you have a good chance of getting a raise? If you do, will it be because you have been promoted? because you have done an outstanding job? because there is a rise in the cost of living? because you got more education?

You are ready to go home now. What time is it? Do you always go home at exactly the same time? Do you have the freedom to decide when to go home? Is there work that you didn't finish today that you decide to take home with you?

What are you thinking about as you go home? Are you preoccupied with something you've been working on? Will you be met by someone when you get home? Will dinner be ready, or will you have to prepare it or help someone prepare it, or wait for someone else to prepare it who is also arriving home from work? Will dinner be sauerkraut in the kitchen, steaks by the pool, or pheasant under glass with aged wine?

With whom will you have dinner: wife, husband, children, members of a communal living arrangement, older relatives who are in your home?

You have now arrived home. What is the neighborhood like in which you live? Is it a bustling city, a pretty suburb, a small town, an isolated rural area? Do you live in an apartment, a room, a row house, a cottage, a farmhouse, a home of your own?

Now you're at dinner. Is the discussion centered around the day's activities with children? about work? about vacation plans? about next weekend's activities? Are you discussing whether the vacation should be a camping trip with the family, a study tour of Europe, or a quiet two weeks at the ocean? Or should the vacation money be spent on home improvement this year? Are you planning a party for the weekend? a camping trip? some work around home? a play and dinner out? a trip on the yacht?

Now that dinner is over, what do you do next? Do you do dishes or read the paper? How will you spend the rest of the evening: sitting in front of the TV, attending a PTA or Scout meeting, helping to plan a community activity, doing some home cleaning or maintenance chores, or finishing some work which you brought home with you?

Your dream day is over now. We hope you enjoyed it . . . and that you can make all of those dreams come true by good career and life planning.

Appendix A
Class Handouts

Career Interests and Skills Assessment Worksheet
The New Frontier
Values Auction

Career Interests and Skills Assessment Worksheet

Instructions: In the spaces in the left column, put in the names of the Life-Career Rainbow roles you are currently playing. In the second column, list interests which are being used in each role. In the third column, list the skills that are being developed and used in each role. In the fourth column, list additional skills that you would like to develop, if any, in these roles.

Roles I Am Playing	Interests I Am Using	Skills I Have Developed	Skills I Want to Develop
Example Student	Reading Having intellectual conversations	Reading fast; comprehending what I read Writing factual reports Computer programming Developing marketing plans	Effective selling Programming microcomputer

The New Frontier

With the advent of the 21st century, the human race is actively pioneering a new frontier—space. The U.S.S. Explorer is about to embark on its mission to establish a colony on Zygor, a small planet located in the far reaches of our galaxy. It has been determined by earlier explorers that Zygor is a habitable planet which possesses all the natural resources necessary to support human life: water, air and fertile soil, as well as abundant plant, marine, and animal life.

Below you will find 14 short descriptions of applicants who are considered suitable for this expedition. Since the spacecraft is limited in size, however, only eight people can be included on the trip to Zygor. Therefore, your task as a member of the selection committee is to determine who will be chosen to be the colonizers. Before making your decision, it is important to know that these first settlers will be supplied regularly from Earth, but there will not be any additional personnel added to this new community for at least 20 years.

Each individual in the group is to take a few minutes to study the list and to select the eight persons you feel should be included on this maiden voyage. Mark your choices in the column labeled "Individual Selections." Next, the group meets for 10-15 minutes to make a group decision. All members of the group must agree on each selection and reach a consensus about their final choices. Now, mark your choices in the column labeled "Group Selections." It is permissible to attempt to influence the rest of the group, but you should also listen carefully to the comments and opinions of others.

	Individual Selections	Group Selections
1. An *agricultural specialist,* who has much information on farming and whose time is spent consulting with farmers about what crops to grow and how to take care of their animals.		
2. An *airline flight attendant* who has lived through a near crash and was cited for bravery in taking care of passengers and staying calm during the near disaster.		
3. A *religious leader,* age in the early 60s, who has served the community for many years and is well liked by its members.		
4. A *construction worker* who works about three or four months out of the year, is a hard worker, and is willing to work whenever a job can be found.		
5. A *U.S. Senator,* age in the early 80s. Before becoming a Senator, he was a lawyer, and in the years in the Senate has served on many committees and has a strong understanding of how the community works.		

6. A *practical nurse* who has had much training and is very good in first aid. _____ _____

7. A *jazz pianist* who is one of the finest musicians in the community. _____ _____

8. A *police officer* who has been very tough and has helped reduce the crime rate. _____ _____

9. A *soldier*—a disabled war veteran who is not able to find employment. _____ _____

10. A *draftsperson* expert in drawing blueprints and other mechanical drawings. _____ _____

11. A *librarian* who is familiar with many books and has read a lot. _____ _____

12. A *social worker* who specializes in family problems and has been a great help to people. _____ _____

13. A *cosmetologist* who is very good at working on both men's and women's hair. _____ _____

14. A *space engineer* who has been active in the space program and knows a lot about all areas of science. _____ _____

Values Auction

Imagine that you are attending an auction of general life- and work-related values. At this auction the bidding must begin at $100 and can only be increased in amounts of $10. Only one person can buy each of the values. You brought $500 specifically for buying at this once-in-a-lifetime opportunity. Review the following list of values which will be on sale; then on the form on the reverse side of this sheet, decide how you will spend your money.

General Life Values

- **Family**—having a warm, pleasant family life with spouse and possibly children
- **Health**—having habitually vibrant health with almost total absence of physical problems
- **Freedom**—being in a country and a home environment which allows the maximum in personal freedom
- **Success**—feeling and having others feel that your life is successful, perhaps including the material possessions to back that up
- **Love**—feeling that you are the most important person in the world to at least one other person and communicating the same feeling to that person
- **Culture**—possessing knowledge and appreciation for music, art, theatre, literature, etc. and having time and money to spend on these things
- **Adventure**—being able to break new exciting trails or to participate in activities with adventure and risk such as mountain climbing, white-water rafting, skiing, hand-gliding, etc.
- **Nature**—having the opportunity to spend time with nature and to enjoy it and communicate with it
- **Productivity**—having a feeling of satisfaction from completing a lot of tasks successfully and making things run smoothly
- **Religion**—being able to hold deep religious beliefs and to commit yourself to them

Work Values

- **High income**—making an income in the top third of the population fairly early in your occupational career
- **Prestige**—having an occupation which society looks up to, such as medical doctor, judge, engineer, etc.
- **Independence**—being able to make most of the decisions about your work tasks and supervising yourself in them
- **Helping others**—being able to contribute to the emotional, physical, and/or educational welfare of people through your occupation

- **Security**—holding a position in which you can be quite sure that you will not be fired or laid off due to change in the economy, automation, or political structure
- **Variety**—being in an occupation which provides a variety of work tasks, perhaps with a variety of kinds of people and in a variety of places
- **Leadership**—being in an occupation which allows you to lead or influence people and policies
- **Leisure**—being in an occupation in which you are not expected to work beyond the usual work hours five days a week, thus providing adequate time for leisure activities
- **Early entry**—getting into an occupation which requires as little training or education as possible

In the following spaces, list the values you would like to buy with your money:

Name of value: **Highest price you would pay:**

_____   _____

_____   _____

_____   _____

_____   _____

                                                     Total $500.00

Appendix B
Paper Graphics

(**Note to course leader:** The following graphics may be photocopied for use as handouts or converted into transparencies for overhead projection. Notes for interpreting Graphic 6, the Career Action Plan map, are found on the reverse side of that graphic.)

1. **Factors in Vocational Maturity**
2. **Impulsive Decider Model**
3. **Super's Developmental Stages and Tasks**
4. **The Life-Career Rainbow**
5. **Holland's Hexagon**
6. **Career Action Plan**
7. **World-of-Work Map with Holland Groups**

Factors in Vocational Maturity

- Awareness of need to plan
- Decision-making skill
- Knowledge and use of resources
- Career information
- Information about World of Work
- Information about preferred occupations

Impulsive Decider 2

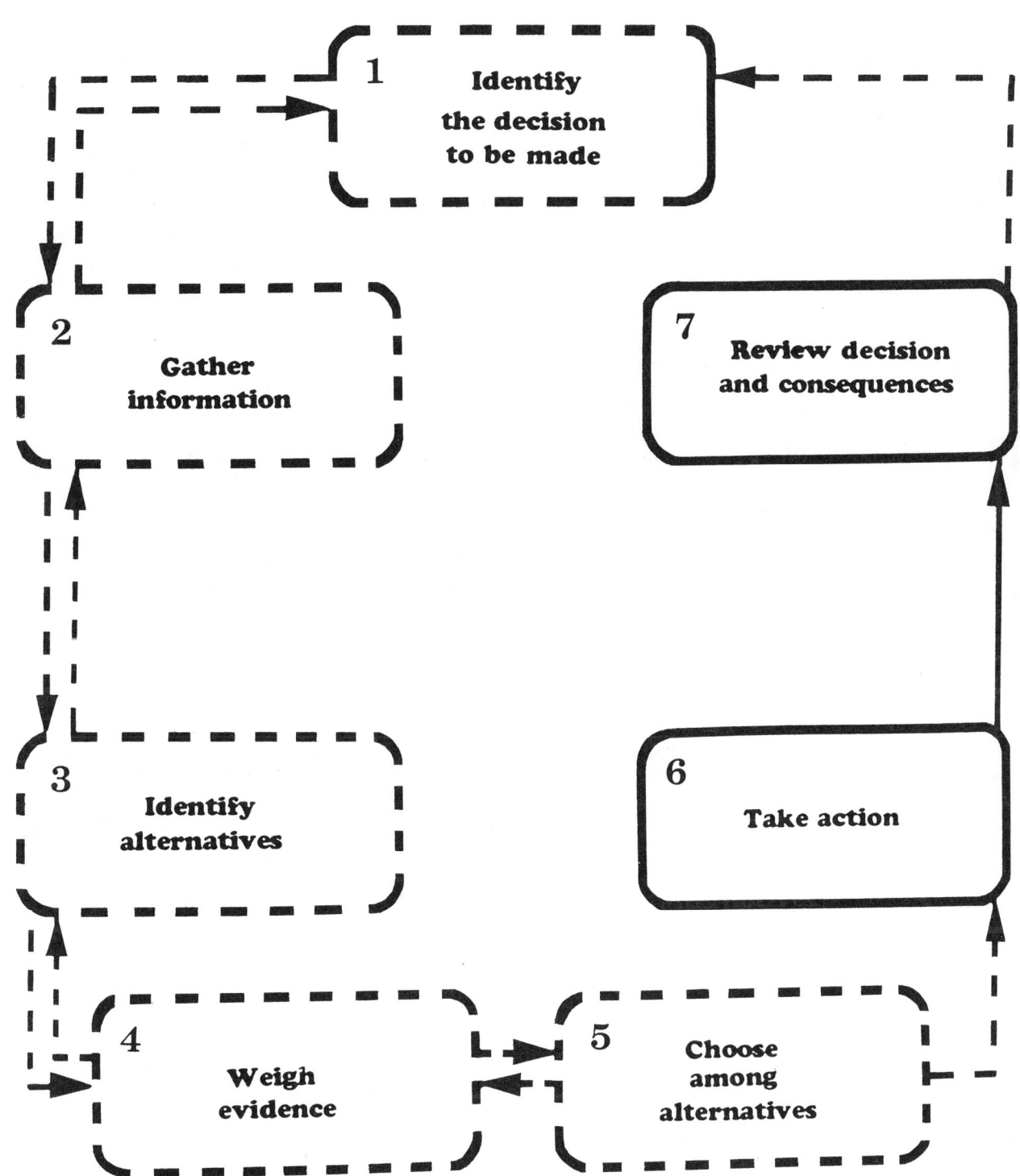

Super's Developmental Stages and Tasks

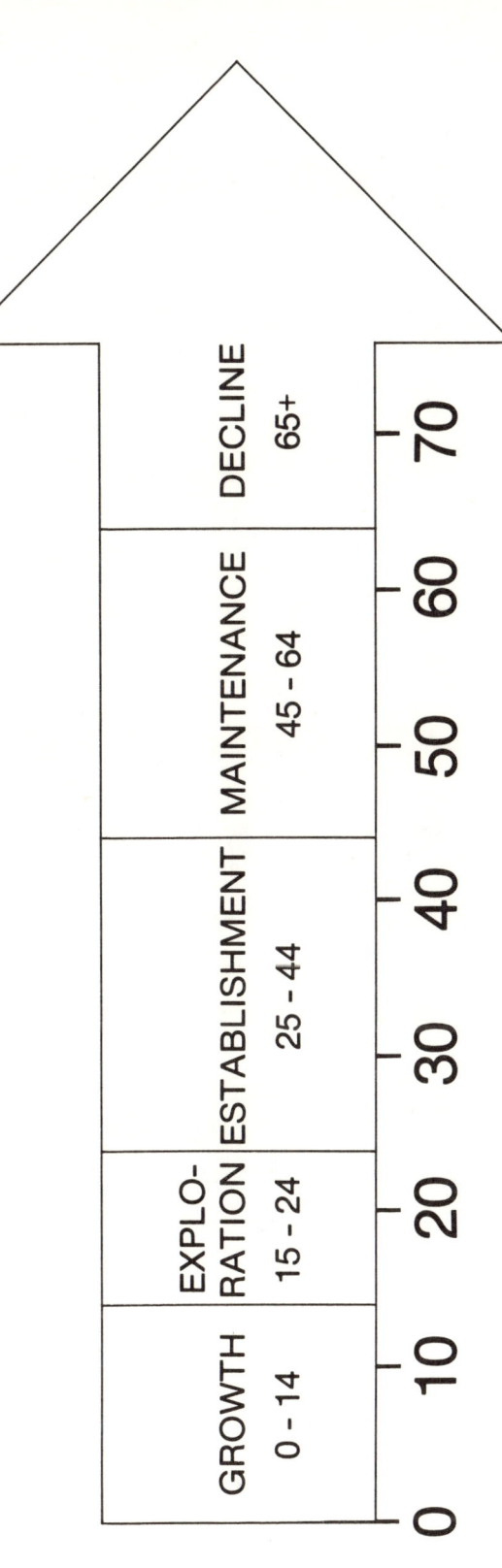

Personal Determinants
Awareness
Attitudes
Interests
Needs-Values
Achievement
General and Specific Aptitudes
Biological Heritage

Situational Determinants, Remote - Immediate
Social Structure
Historical Change
Socioeconomic Organization and Conditions
Employment Practices
School
Community
Family

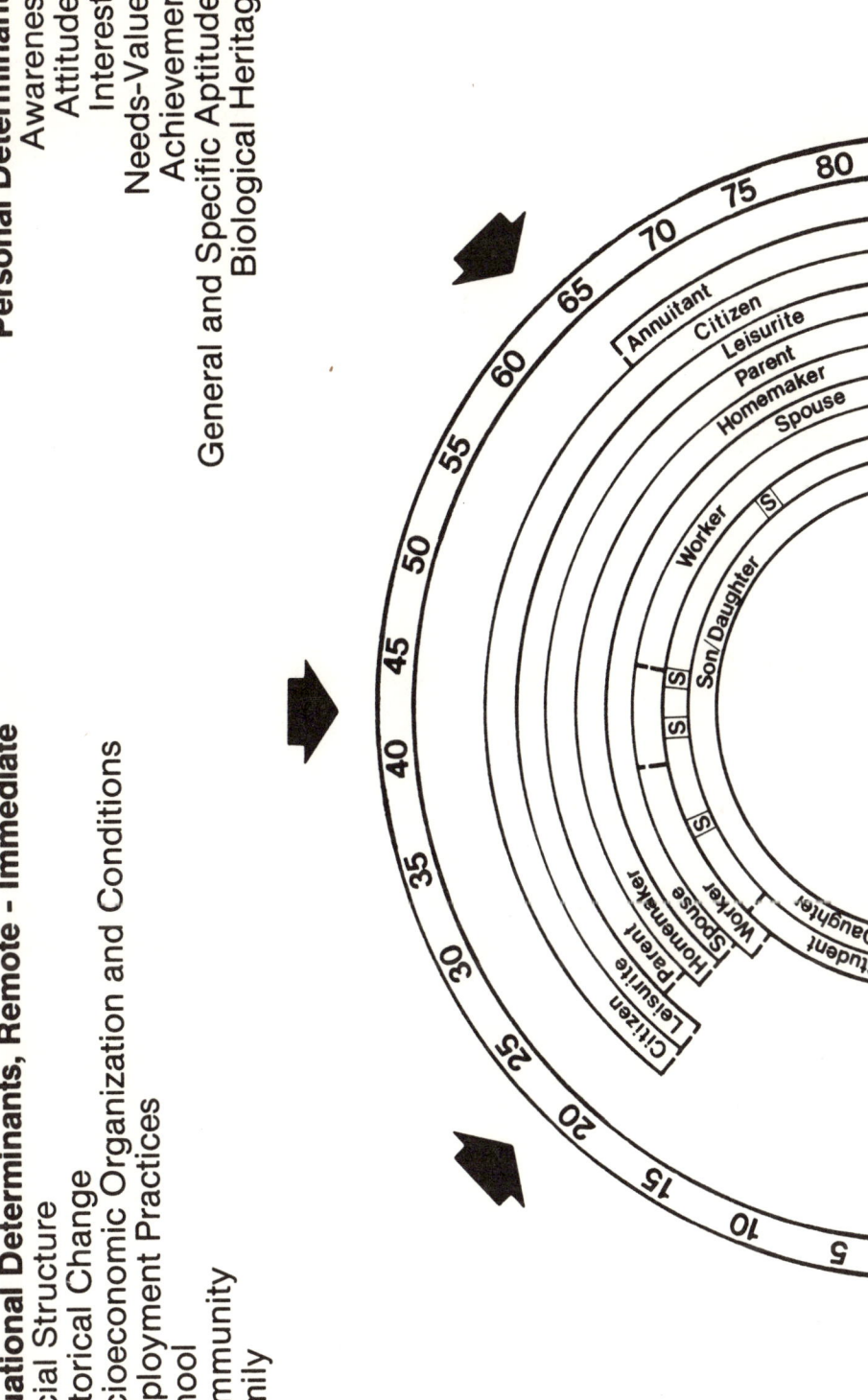

The Life-Career Rainbow: Nine life roles in schematic life space.

Hexagon Showing Relationships among Holland's Six Work Environments

5

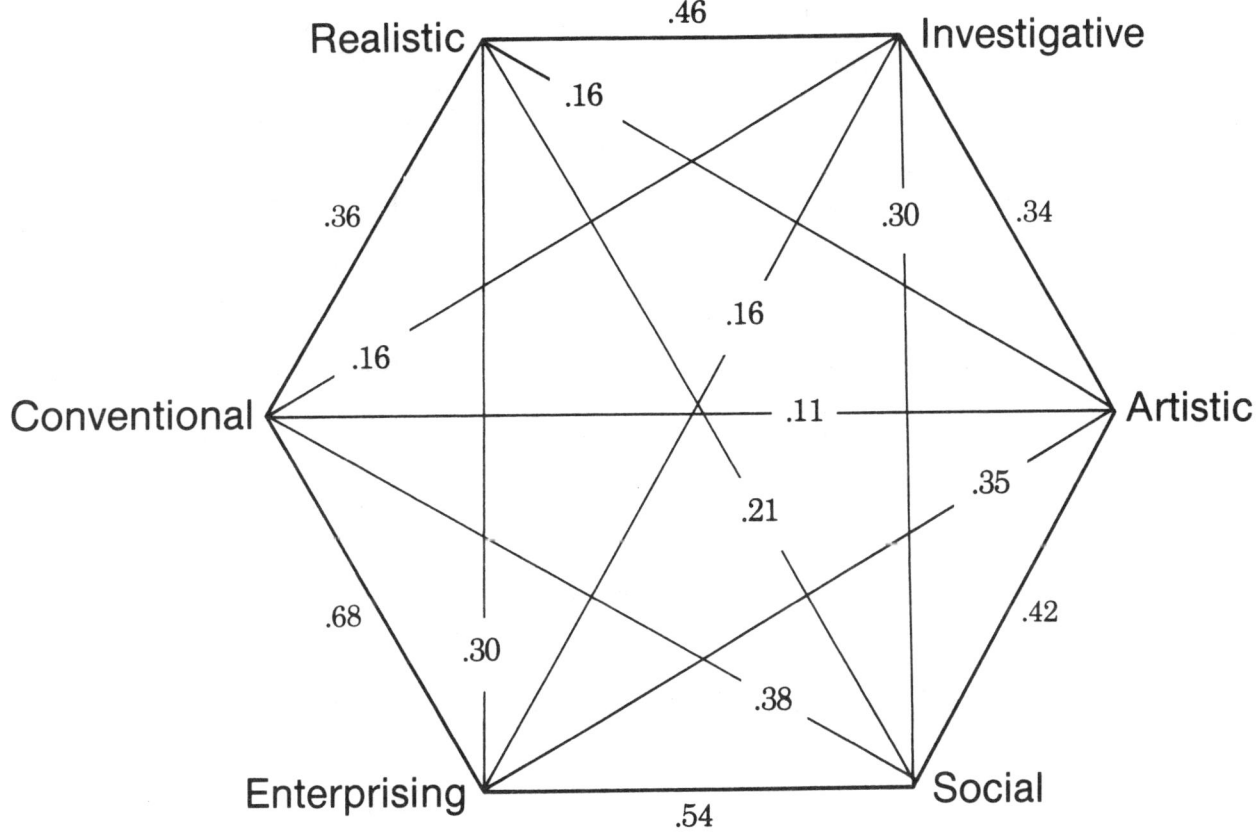

Source: J. L. Holland, D. R. Whitney, N. S. Cole, and J. M. Richards, Jr. *An empirical occupational classification derived from a theory of personality and intended for practice and research,* ACT Research Report No. 29, Iowa City, Iowa: The American College Testing Program, 1969.

OCCUPATIONAL GOAL:

- Job market ③
- Grad school
- Transfer program
- Occupational curricula
- Enter or continue community college
- Enter technical or specialized school for training
- Enter the military for training and/or career
- Enter apprenticeship for training
- Enter or continue four year college or university
- Job market
- Go to job market
- ② GET FURTHER EDUCATION OR TRAINING
- Still undecided
- ① Where do I go from here?
- START

Career Action Plan

133

The "Career Action Plan" map shows most of the alternatives which you have for your next action steps. From road sign 1 you have the alternatives of (a) still undecided, (b) getting further education or training, or (c) going to the job market. If you choose to get further education or training, you have at least five alternatives: (a) apprenticeship, (b) military, (c) technical or specialized school, (d) community college, or (e) four-year college. After completing four-year college, you can choose between entering the job market or going to graduate school—or you may combine the two. After two-year college, you may choose between transferring to a four-year college or entering the job market.

World-of-Work Map
with Holland Groups

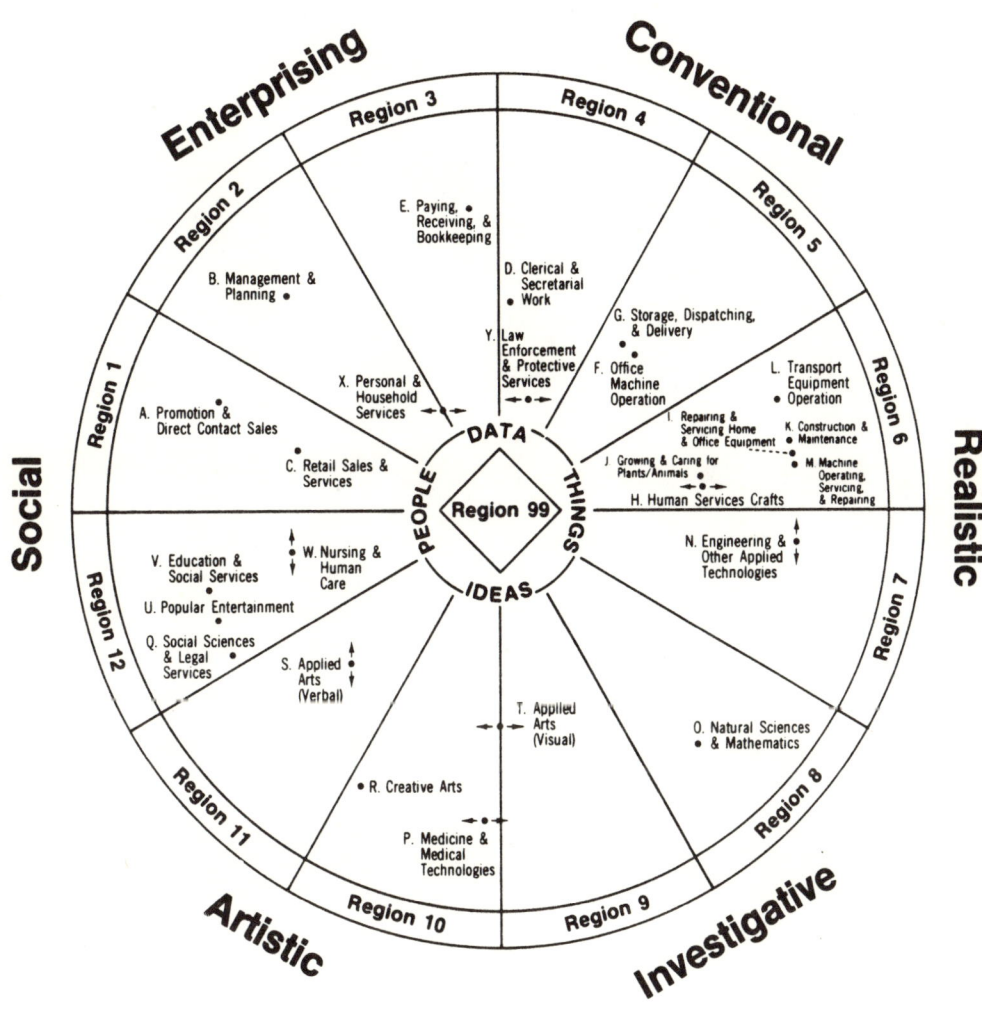

Appendix C
Exercise 4B—Exploring Occupations by Assessing Your Interests
(Alternative to Exercise 4A)

In Exercise 4A of the *Career Planning Guide,* participants complete the abbreviated, 60-item version of UNIACT to determine the World-of-Work Map region most consistent with their interests. The scoring provides no other report of UNIACT results. Participants completing this alternative exercise take the complete, 90-item version of UNIACT, the scoring of which yields both a World-of-Work Map region and scores on six scales corresponding to the Holland types. Thus, group leaders who wish to provide guidance based on Holland scores and/or codes should substitute this exercise for Exercise 4A.

In this exercise, participants find their World-of-Work Map region in a table that relates Holland codes to region numbers. This process is somewhat less precise than the more direct procedure of Exercise 4A. Consequently, if a group completes both exercises (which would be inefficient), the regions obtained by a few individuals may not agree. (Lack of perfectly reliable measures will also contribute to differences.) For most of these individuals, however, the two regions will be adjacent.

Low-consistency profiles, which suggest unusual combinations of divergent interests, present a special challenge for interpretation. Such profiles are flagged in Table C.2, which students use to obtain a World-of-Work Map region from their three-letter Holland code. Both the footnote to that table and the scoring instructions provided below suggest that participants with low-consistency profiles request assistance in interpreting their entire profile. By examining all six scores, you may be able to suggest specific occupations which integrate these divergent interests. Indeed, obtaining information necessary to provide such assistance is a primary reason for selecting this alternate exercise. In Exercise 4A, many participants with low-consistency profiles receive Region "?" scores, and therefore receive no benefit from UNIACT; others obtain only the region which is the best single resolution of their divergent interests.

Since scoring of this alternate exercise is more complex than that of Exercise 4A, and leader assistance is needed to interpret that additional score information, the *Guide* does not provide scoring instructions. The leader must, therefore, guide the participants through the scoring process, step by step.

Before leading the group through the scoring instructions, explain why you assigned this exercise instead of Exercise 4A. If possible, prepare overhead projector transparencies of UNIACT, and Tables C.1 and C.2. As you read the instructions, project the appropriate transparency and clarify the directions with examples.

Scoring Instructions

Step 1—Obtain the raw scores for your Holland scales.

a. For each of the six scales, count the number of "L" responses and enter this total in the box beneath the "L" column. Similarly, enter the number of "D" responses beneath the "D" column. Ignore the "I" column.

b. For each of the six scales, perform the computation indicated under the response columns: 15 + (number of "L" responses) − (number of "D" responses) = score. Your score can range from 0 (if you marked "D" to all items) to 30 (if you marked "L" to all items). (*Note to leader.* You may wish to show an example on the transparency or blackboard: 15 + **7** − **4** = 18. Also, you may wish to do spot checks of the participants' computations.)

Step 2—Plot your profile.

a. In Table C.1, find your score on the R scale in the column labeled R. Circle this number. Similarly, circle your I-scale score under the column labeled I, etc.

b. Draw a straight line from the circled number under the R-scale heading to the circled number under the I-scale heading; draw another straight line from the circled number under the I-scale heading to the circled number under the A-scale heading; etc. The resulting graph is your interest profile.

Step 3—Find your three-letter code.

a. On the graph you just drew on Table C.1, note where the peak occurs. (Ignore the values of the numbers; just note which circle is nearest the top.) The letter for that scale is the first letter of your three-letter code.

b. Note which scales have the second and third highest peaks. The letters for these scales are the second and third letters of your code.

c. Record your three-letter code in the blank to the right of the graph.

d. If the first two of your top three scores are equally or nearly equally high on the graph, also record the code or codes obtained by reversing the order of these tied scores. If, for example, your I and R scales are equally high on the graph, and S is the third highest, enter both IRS and RIS codes. If all three of your top three scores are equally high, do not enter any code. Instead, when time permits, ask for assistance in interpreting your entire profile. (*Note to leader.* One standard error of measurement—SEM—on Table C.1 is approximately one-half inch. Thus, scores may be considered to be similar if they differ by less than one inch on the vertical dimension. When this happens, the standard error bands overlap.)

Step 4—Find your World-of-Work Map region number.

a. From Table C.2 find the World-of-Work Map region that corresponds to your three-letter code. If you obtained more than one three-letter code (due to ties or near ties), find all corresponding regions.

b. Enter the region(s) in the blanks on page 147.

c. A code marked with an "a" superscript suggests an unusual combination of interests. By interpreting your entire profile, your leader may be able to suggest other regions—and possibly some specific occupations—that correspond to your combination of scores. When time permits, ask your leader for assistance.

Step 5—Record your results on the World-of-Work Map on pages 125.

On that map, place an "I" (for "interests") in the region(s) you just obtained.

Appendix D
Course Syllabus Chart

Session Number	Content	Step of Decision-making Process	Suggested Activity/ Homework Due	Date of Session
1	Overview of program Administration of evaluation instrument Introduction to decision making			
2	Decision-making problems Group decision-making experience	Step 1: Identifying the problem	Read Chapters 1 and 2 of the *Career Planning Guide*. Complete Exercise 1, Decisions List, to be handed in.	
3	Life-career rainbow	Step 1	Read Chapter 3 of the *Career Planning Guide*.	
4	Self-concept and career implications	Step 2: Gathering information about self and environment	Read Chapter 4 of the *Career Planning Guide*. Complete Exercise 3, Vocational Self-Concept Questionnaire. Begin to read biography or autobiography of a famous person.	
5	Organization of World of Work Internal factors influencing vocational choice: interests and skills	Step 2	Read Chapter 5 of the *Career Planning Guide*. Complete Exercise 4A. Continue reading biography or autobiography and write report (due in this session).	
6	Internal factors influencing vocational choice: abilities	Step 2	Complete Exercise 5, Exploring Occupations by Assessing your Experience and Skills, of the *Career Planning Guide*.	
7	Identifying occupations related to personal interests, abilities, and skills, and experiences	Step 2	Score CPP Abilities Test	
8	External factors influencing vocational choice: stereotypes	Step 2	Read Chapter 7 of the *Career Planning Guide,* and complete Exercise 6, Stereotyping in Employment, with either of the two options described.	

(Continued)

Syllabus Chart—*Continued*

Session Number	Content	Step of Decision-making Process	Suggested Activity/ Homework Due	Date of Session
9	External factors influencing vocational choice: career information	Step 3: Identifying alternatives	Read Chapter 8 of the *Career Planning Guide*.	
10	Occupational research	Step 4: Weighing the evidence	Complete Exercise 8, Occupational Research Sheet, of the *Career Planning Guide* for five occupations.	
11	Occupational interviews	Step 4	Interview at least one of the two people listed on the Occupational Research Plan Sheet. Use Exercise 9, the Occupational Interview Sheet, for doing so. Be prepared to discuss this interview in the next class session.	
12	Narrowing occupational alternatives	Step 5: Choosing among alternatives	Work on final projects.	
13	Career Action Plan Identify major or program of study Resume writing	Step 6: Taking action	Read Chapters 9 and 10. Complete Exercise 10, Preferred Job Characteristics and Values, of the *Career Planning Guide*.	
14	Review of program	Step 7: Reviewing the decision and consequences	Prepare to give oral report to class on individual project. Write up project to hand in.	
15	Final exam (if desired)			

References

Blau, P. H., Parnes, H. S., Gustad, J. W., Jessor, R., & Wilcox, R. C. Occupational Choice: A Conceptual Framework. *Industrial and Labor Relations,* 1956, *9,* No. 4, 531-543.

Crites, J. O. The Career Maturity Inventory. In D. E. Super (Ed.), *Measuring Vocational Maturity for Counseling and Evaluation.* Washington, D.C.: National Vocational Guidance Association, 1974, 25-39.

Dinklage, L. B. *Adolescent Choice and Decision Making: A Review of Decision-Making Models and Issues in Relation to Some Developmental Tasks of Adolescence.* Cambridge, Mass.: Harvard University, 1966 (ERIC Document Reproduction Service No. ED 010 371).

Friedman, F. A. & Havighurst, R. J. *The Meaning of Work and Retirement.* Chicago: University of Chicago Press, 1954.

Harren, V. A. A model of career decision making for college students. *Journal of Vocational Behavior,* 1979, *14,* 119-133.

Havighurst, R. J. *Human Development and Education.* Longmans, Green, and Company, 1953.

Havighurst, R. J., Bowman, P. H., Liddle, G. F., Mathews, C. V., & Pierce, J. V. *Growing Up in River City.* New York: John Wiley and Sons, 1962.

Hilton, T. J. Career Decision Making. *Journal of Counseling Psychology,* 1962, *9,* 291-298.

Holland, J. L. *Making Vocational Choices.* Englewood Cliffs, N.J.: Prentice Hall, 1973.

Jordaan, J. P. & Super, D. E. The Prediction of Early Adult Behavior. In D. F. Ricks, A. Thomas, & M. Ross (Eds.), Chapter 6 of *Life History Research in Psychopathology.* Minneapolis: University of Minnesota Press, 1974.

Lamb, R. R. & Prediger, D. J. *Technical Report for the Unisex Edition of the ACT Interest Inventory (UNIACT).* Iowa City, Iowa: The American College Testing Program, 1981.

O'Tolle, J. et al. *Work in America.* Cambridge, Mass: MIT Press, 1973.

Roe, A. *Psychology of Occupations.* New York: John Wiley and Sons, 1956.

Smith, D. *A Review of the Literature of Decision Making.* Charleston, W.Va.: Appalachia Educational Laboratory, 1972.

Steer, R. A. The Relationship between Satisfaction with Retirement and Similarity of Self-ratings for Past Occupations and Present Activities of Educators. (Unpublished doctoral dissertation, Teachers College, Columbia University, 1970.)

Super, D. E. *The Psychology of Careers.* New York: Harper and Brothers, 1957.

Super, D. E. Vocational Maturity Theory: Toward Implementing a Psychology of Career Education and Guidance. In D. E. Super (Ed.), *Measuring Vocational Maturity for Counseling and Evaluation.* Washington, D.C.: National Vocational Guidance Association, 1974, 9-24.

Super, D. E. How people make and might be helped to make career choices. Paper presented at the CRAC/NICEC Seminar held at King's College, Cambridge, July 1975.

Super, D. E. A Life-Span, Life-Space Approach to Career Development. *Journal of Vocational Behavior,* 1980, *16,* 282-298.

Super, D. E., Kowalski, R. S., & Gotkin, E. H. *Floundering and Trial after High School.* New York: Teachers College, 1967 (mimeographed).

Super, D. E., Starishevsky, R., Matlin, N., & Jordaan, J. P. *Career Develoment: Self-Concept Theory.* Princeton, N.J.: College Entrance Examination Board, 1963.

Thompson, A. S. & Lindeman, R. H. *Career Development Inventory, Volume 1: User's Manual.* Palo Alto, California: Consulting Psychologists Press, 1981.

Tiedeman, D. V. & Miller, A. L. Decision Making for the 70s: The Cubing of the Tiedeman Paradigm and Its Application in Career Education. *Focus on Guidance,* September 1972, *5* (1).

Tiedeman, D. V. & O'Hara, R. P. *Career Development: Choice and Adjustment.* New York: College Entrance Examination Board, 1963.

Notes

Notes

Notes

Notes